THE PILGRIM

AND

THE PILGRIMAGE

THE PILGRIM
AND
THE PILGRIMAGE

Emily B. Sellon

Published and distributed
with the generous support of
John A. Sellon
and his sons,
Peter, Jeffrey, and Michael

Olcott Institute of the
Theosophical Society in America and
The Theosophical Publishing House
Wheaton, Illinois / Madras, India

For additional information, write to

The Theosophical Society in America
P. O. Box 270
Wheaton, IL 60189-0270

First Edition 1996

Library of Congress Cataloging-in-Publication Data

Sellon, Emily B., 1908–1993.
   The pilgrim and the pilgrimage / Emily B. Sellon. — 1st ed.

      p.   cm. — (Wisdom tradition books ; 1)
   Includes bibliographical references (p.).
   ISBN 0-8356-0752-6
   1. Theosophy.   2. Metaphysics.   3. Spiritual life.   I. Title.
II. Series.
BP565.S36P55   1996
299'.934 — dc20   96-16233
                                                                              CIP

5 4 3 2 1 * 96 97 98 99 00 01 02

Printed in the United States of America

WISDOM TRADITION BOOKS

A Series Edited by John Algeo

This series of books is published for and dedicated to Theosophical students at all levels of study. It includes new works on the Wisdom Tradition, which is Theosophy, presenting the timeless truths of ancient seers in modern idiom; reprints and new editions of older works that contain much of relevance to readers of all times; and historical and reference works relating to Theosophy and the Theosophical Society.

Scheduled books in the series include the following:

1. *The Pilgrim and the Pilgrimage*, by Emily Sellon

2. *A Catalog of Books Belonging to H. P. Blavatsky*, by Michael Gomes

3. *The Peopling of the Earth*, by Geoffrey A. Barborka

Contents

Foreword

In *The Key to Theosophy*, H. P. Blavatsky wrote, "Theosophist is, who Theosophy does." By that definition, Emily Sellon was one of our premier Theosophists. For many of those who knew her, Emily remains their model of what a Theosophist should do and be.

Emily was active in the New York Lodge, Pumpkin Hollow Farm, the Northeast Federation, the national Society, and the international Society. She entered wholeheartedly into the life of the Society: meditating, studying, teaching, writing, editing, decorating, gardening, and cooking for hungry crowds. But most important, she was a Theosophist in her very nature, and thus she lived Theosophy day to day.

Emily had a big view of Theosophy. No narrow-minded partisan, she saw in the great principles of *The Secret Doctrine* not just a theory of cosmogenesis and anthropogenesis, but a practical guide to living. For her, theory and practice were an integral whole. She lived what she believed.

Emily's last public teaching was a weekend seminar on "The Pilgrim and the Pilgrimage," which she led at Pumpkin Hollow Farm just ten days before she died. It was a summation of her integrative view of Theosophical theory and practice. The audio tapes of that workshop are available from Pumpkin Hollow Farm, which has also published excerpts from the workshop in pamphlet form.

This volume has been edited from a transcription of the Pumpkin Hollow tapes kindly made by Ann M. and

Douglas L. Clemens. It is offered as a concise statement of Emily's philosophy and of the metaphysical foundation of Theosophy.

Born on October 10, 1908, Emily Boenke joined the Theosophical Society through the Service Lodge of New York at the age of 20 in April 1929. Her sponsors were Captain Ernest M. Sellon and his daughter, Elizabeth Sellon. In 1931 Emily married John Sellon, son of Captain Ernest and Mrs. Barbara A. Sellon, two very active and dedicated members of the Society. During the sixty-two years of John and Emily's marriage, they too were active Theosophists, citizens, and parents, raising three sons. The birth of the eldest, Peter, on June 30, 1934, was announced in the *American Theosophist* for September of that year. Michael and Jeffrey followed.

Soon after her entry into the Society, Emily became active as a Theosophical leader, teacher, and supporter, especially in the New York Lodge, which united three earlier Lodges (New York, Service, and Central), and the Northeast Federation. Her first work for the Society was to catalog the library of the New York Lodge, a task that she said "opened up to her the entire body of theosophical writings" (AT 63 [1975]: 55). She served as corresponding secretary of the Lodge during 1938–1941 and 1942–1945, when presidents of the New York Lodge were Will Ross, John Sellon, and Dora Kunz, and again later for a period after 1974.

Emily was herself president of the New York Lodge during 1950–1954 and 1964–1968. In her presidential terms, she was instrumental in acquiring and remodeling a building for the Lodge on East 53 Street and in founding the New York Quest Bookshop there. She was a regular lecturer at the New York Lodge, Pumpkin Hollow, the Section's annual meeting and summer school, the Krotona School, and various lodges around the country.

Among the many administrative positions Emily held in the national Section, she was chair of a Committee on the New Socio-Economic Plan, reporting on the committee's work in the *American Theosophist* of November 1940 (246–8). She served as Director from the Northeast District for two terms during the presidency of James Perkins (1954 to 1960) and for one during the presidency of Dora Kunz (1975 to 1978), and as National First Vice President for two terms (1978 to 1984).

In the mid 1950s, Emily and Joy Mills inaugurated the work of the Research Division of the Education Department, and Emily continued to give it her attention for many years. She was also the long-serving chair of the National Education Committee, a group consisting of professionals and Theosophical teachers. Under her guidance, that committee produced the "Theosophical Worldview" statement, which has been published in the *American Theosophist* since August/September 1982 and has been widely adopted around the world.

Emily's international work included fifteen years of service, from January 1978 to December 1992, as an Additional Member on the General Council, the chief governing body of the Theosophical Society. Those years fell within the presidencies of John Coats and Radha Burnier. Emily also served from 1978 to 1980 on the General Council's

Committee on Structure and Procedures. Her international lecturing included Australia and India.

In addition to working directly for the Society, Emily devoted about thirty years of her life to the journal *Main Currents in Modern Thought*. Fritz Kunz began the publication in November 1940 as "a monthly report on all items of a certain significance . . . which have appeared in some 2,000 English language journals and books during the prior month." It was to provide summaries, reviews, and commentaries for current information.

The first two volumes of *Main Currents* were mimeographed on variously colored paper: green for biology and psychobiology of living creatures of every kind, pink for human psychobiology, blue for anthropology, orange for social man, yellow for physical sciences, and white for "basic methods" such as mathematics, principles of art, and linguistics. A prominent early contributor and co-founder was Benjamin Lee Whorf, a linguist whose theory about the relationship between language and thought still intrigues many students of language.

By volume 3 (beginning November 1942), *Main Currents* was professionally printed on white stock, and original articles, rather than summaries and brief commentary, were becoming the staple of the magazine. After the fifth and last issue of that volume in March 1943, there was a hiatus until volume 4, number 1, appeared in January 1944, followed by another long hiatus.

The December 1945 *American Theosophist* carried an article by Emily Sellon, secretary of the new Committee on Integration, which recently elected National President

James Perkins had appointed. The committee's charge was to work for the integration of Theosophy and modern knowledge in a variety of ways, including the resumption of publication of *Main Currents in Modern Thought*. The content of the journal was not to be "specifically Theosophical in its terminology," although "all material of course will document our philosophy in some particular field, since that is the basis upon which our work is done."

The magazine resumed publication in April 1946, when "E. B. Sellon" appears on the publisher's page as Associate Editor. In the December 1946 *American Theosophist*, John Sellon outlined the work of the Integration Committee and was able to report the completion of the fourth volume of *Main Currents*. In October 1947, the magazine announced the formation of the Foundation for Integrated (later Integrative) Education, which, like *Main Currents*, became an intellectual force in its time.

During the thirty-five years of its existence, *Main Currents* had a distinguished roster of contributors, some of the well-known names being Fritjof Capra, Buckminster Fuller, Lama Anagarika Govinda, Henry Margenau, Jacob Needleman, F. S. C. Northrop, Linus Pauling, Ira Progoff, J. B. Rhine, Henryk Skolimowski, Huston Smith, Pitirim A. Sorokin, Arnold Toynbee, Earl Warren, Renée Weber, and Ken Wilber. At the beginning of volume 26 in 1969, Emily Sellon and Henry Margenau became coeditors with Fritz Kunz and continued jointly as editors after Fritz's death.

The magazine ceased publication in 1975 with a retrospective issue that is still a collector's item. In it Emily summarized the philosophy of *Main Currents* and her own view on life as well:

All true knowledge arises from the integration of two domains of knowing—the perceptual, aesthetic and experiential, and the abstract, theoretical, or conceptual. Both these modes must be nurtured if we are to achieve personal integration and wholeness; both are essential for the growth and renewal of our culture.

Integration was the keynote of *Main Currents*, as it was of the rest of Fritz Kunz's and Emily Sellon's work. As her memorial notice in *The Quest* magazine put it:

The integrative approach of *Main Currents* expressed the harmony Emily Sellon believed underlies the visible and subtle universe. Her conviction was that all visible forms are the outer expression of an inner spiritual consciousness. To those who knew her, it was clear that this feeling was palpably real. It accounted for her rapport with plants and animals, for her sensitivity to beauty and her talent for creating it, and for her empathy with people.

Emily's editorial skills were not limited to *Main Currents*. She edited several of Dora Kunz's books published by the Theosophical Publishing House and made a significant contribution to Theosophical literature as a publishing consultant and editor. She was always ready to be of assistance to other writers, and her keen sense of style as well as her deep knowledge of Theosophy were invaluable. When I drafted a pamphlet on the cult phenomena, I sent it to Emily a few months before her death. She and Renée Weber, who was visiting Emily at the time, went over the manuscript with the intelligence and dedication that characterized all her work. She sent me a response almost as long as the original, as a result of which the final version was considerably improved.

Among her many activities, Emily served on the Board of the Happy Valley Foundation in Ojai, California, which operates the Happy Valley School. That school, founded by Krishnamurti, Aldous Huxley, and others, was intended to realize a vision of Annie Besant's. Emily was also active as a community member in the Rye, New York, area, serving with a philanthropic group, the Tenth Twig, in support of the United Hospital of Port Chester.

Emily's charitable activities were by no means limited to corporate ones. She followed the injunction found in both the Gospels and H. P. Blavatsky's writings to do good deeds quietly, directly, and personally. Few knew of the extensive help she gave to others—physically, mentally, and spiritually—and certainly she never spoke of it. For Emily, to do good works was natural and inevitable. Her actions were the expression of her being.

Emily was that rare combination of Mary and Martha in one. As intellectual as were her Theosophical interests, she did not hesitate to deal with the nitty-gritty of everyday affairs. Emily Sellon was one of the founders of Pumpkin Hollow Farm, and as such her role was not merely that of directing and supporting. Emily did the tough physical work along with everyone to establish the Hollow as a vibrant, effective center of Theosophical work.

Always close to her family, Emily lived to enjoy several grandchildren. She was known for creating beautiful interiors in her home and at Theosophical sites. She was a cook of no mean ability. In 1942 she compiled a book of gourmet vegetarian recipes, *From Hand to Mouth,* which was published by the Theosophical Press in Wheaton, a precursor of the present Theosophical Publishing House, with a foreword by her dear friend Otelia J. Bengtsson, a medical doctor. It is a typically Emilyish work in combining a philosophical concern for the sanctity of life, practical attention to diet and health, and an aesthetic devotion to good taste (in several senses of that word). Its recipes range from avocado cocktail to orange pecan muffins, and are liberally seasoned with thyme, parsley, cinnamon, nutmeg, cloves, ginger, basil, bay, dill, chives, leeks, mint, mustard, sage, summer savory, and garlic.

Emily died in Theosophical peacefulness on October 27, 1993, a few weeks after her eighty-fifth birthday, surrounded by family: her husband, John, and their three sons, Peter, Michael, and Jeffrey. A memorial service was held at the New York Lodge on November 6 attended by her family, friends, colleagues, and admirers. The epigraph for the announcement of that service summarizes what many have felt about her:

Emily's kindness, sense of humor, and dedication to the Theosophical ideals of human unity have deeply touched us. We have been changed for the better in knowing her.

Renée Weber spoke of Emily at that service, as a friend and colleague. Her eulogy follows.

John Algeo

In Memory of Emily Sellon

Emily Sellon's life was shaped by love and unified in beauty. It was so remarkably fulfilled, so gifted and varied, enveloped by such abundant love, that it might have been several lives at once. This multilayered life was necessary to Emily, for she could settle for nothing less than an active relationship to the mystery of the vast universe. What her depth made necessary, her vitality made possible. Emily was blessed with a rare and seemingly inexhaustible energy on which she drew confidently and which remained with her to the end of her life. I believe, as she did, that it was the energy of love.

Her love expressed itself in action in many forms: devotion, support, friendship, dedication, companionship, altruism, selflessness, practical help; it could move from awe to wit or whimsy—whatever seemed appropriate. Emily's love radiated to her close-knit family and to the human family as a whole, to the world of plants and animals, to philosophical principles from East and West, and above all to Theosophy. It was the center of her spiritual life, its inspiration since her girlhood when—as she put it—she fell irrevocably in love with it at her very first encounter. In its study, teaching, writing, and practical activities she found inspiration, challenge, and fulfillment; her audiences caught the enthusiasm, grateful for her erudition and her tireless dedication.

Through her Theosophical life she became associated with Fritz Kunz, a kindred spirit who inspired Emily for the decades she worked with him in various capacities on *Main*

Currents in Modern Thought and with whom she could pursue the integration of the great theosophical principles which they brought into the age of science, and with Greek theosophical predecessors. Emily was also close to Dora Kunz, one of her most trusted friends, and helped give birth to Dora's books on healing and the human energy field. As President and Vice President of the Theosophical Society in America, Dora and Emily initiated many novel events.

Although it was a group venture, Emily was instrumental in formulating "The Theosophical World View," an eloquent condensation of the essence of Theosophy. To share just one phrase with you, here is her elegant credo near the end of the document. "Devotion to truth, love for all living beings, and commitment to a life of active altruism are the marks of the true Theosophist." This credo was part of her and by it she lived her life.

I have said that Emily's life was shaped by love and unified in beauty, and so it was. Her search for their integration ran like a melody through her life. Before I share that perception with you, for it captured something utterly fundamental in Emily's spirit, I want to turn aside from these high planes to evoke another, more personal side of my mentor and friend. For my friend she was! How blessed am I in these twenty-some years of closeness with her. My delight in her being grew, and I never tired of talking with her. We went on for hours on subjects serious and even frivolous, for her sense of humor was fantastic. Sometimes John would come in, feigning astonishment: "Are you two still at it?" he would ask, knowing full well that as far as we were concerned, we had scarcely begun a conversation that could have no real end. We talked on land, in water, in the air at 30,000 feet, and even under water, in the delight of snorkeling which Emily taught me.

We enjoyed writing together. The same intensity, concentration, pleasure and—yes, fun—characterized our joint articles and other writings, lectures for symposia and conferences, book chapters, traveling together. Emily made everything seem special. She had the gift of investing anything she did with weight and meaning. Nothing was ever mundane to her, everything glowed and was special, luminous under her tutelage. She stamped it all with an immediacy and a contagious sense of adventure.

To many of us, she embodied the beauty and harmony, the elegance and simplicity, that she found in the great Platonic ideas. As above, so below. The hermetic dictum. The messenger became the embodiment, perfect or less than perfect: what did it matter when her irrepressible spirit lavished itself on the beauty she perceived?

Hers was a life shaped by love and unified by beauty. And so I turn to beauty, for this, too, contains the essence of the Emily I knew. She saw beauty as realized or as potential in all things, and where it was lacking, she created it herself, with her artistic talent and taste. But lest we misunderstand her, the beauty she sought and saw was no mere aestheticism, and her lifelong work on its behalf was no random busyness. What she shaped with love was the inner essence of beauty expressed in outer form. A beauty that existed beyond matter, time, and space. For Emily beauty evoked the other great Platonic realities, the true and the good, expressing the timeless in time.

Her window on the world was beauty. Through it she saw the spiritual source expressing itself in the material. To her, they were one. When Emily nurtured her garden, fed her birds or wild swans, and created environments of harmony, order, and peace, she was not decorating but making visible the great invisible universals that to her were reality itself. In nature, art, artifacts, ideas, and people, she saw the true and the good. For if her window was beauty, what she perceived through it she perceived with nonjudgmental eyes. Her compassionate spirit seldom forgot that it had chosen the path of love.

Emily was not sentimental. Hers was a vision akin to the pure vision of the mathematician, who sees truth in the beauty of his equations. So it was with her. Beauty was but the beginning; the inner essence of it she knew best in meditation, a profound center of her life on which she chose to remain mostly silent.

The energy of Emily's love gave one a sense of well-being. A stay with her and John was a gift: it nourished physically, intellectually, and spiritually. The sacred and the daily were interwoven, and one felt complete. "Man is a plant, whose roots are up in heaven." Plato's description fits Emily well. She loved the earthy flower she planted and nourished and the transcendent reality that made its existence possible.

One facet of Emily's personality that revealed the depth of her spiritual aspirations was her diffidence. Despite her strong personality that thrust countless leadership roles on her, Emily often told me that her ardent wish in this life was to dwell in the background. A learning experience which she had set for herself, she espoused it with her whole being.

This diffidence I see as a paradox, weaving its way through her life. It is as if she wanted to disappear into the great principles that she taught, wanted to become transparent to them, so that others would see the teachings and not her. But this was not to be. The more she tried to become transparent to the ideas, the more we saw the ideas because of Emily. Hence we perceived her in all her shimmering beauty and goodness, the one who made these wonders come alive for us. We loved her all the more because in those difficult and exalting discourses, the bridge was Emily.

Her form is gone, but she believed with all her being that the inner essence outlasts the form; that the spirit is made of stuff so powerful and subtle that nothing can destroy it; that it exists beyond time and death, transcending both in its continuing journey; and that nothing can part those who love one another, for love, she said, is the strongest force there is. And though I shall miss her painfully, I know that the timeless self of Emily is here, is now, is with us still, and continues to enrich our lives.

Renée Weber

1. Metaphysics and Machinery

What we are going to talk about is essentially metaphysics. In Theosophical studies there are really two approaches. One is metaphysics or the "grand principles," and the other is what I call "machinery." That may seem like a derogatory or pejorative term, but nevertheless that is what it really is. Studies of reincarnation and karma, or of the cycles and rounds and races and that kind of thing, are really studies of the machinery, that is, the consequences of the working out of metaphysical principles.

Most people are usually content to study only the machinery because from it you can gain a great deal that is relevant to your own experience. You can see it working out in your own life. The insight that studying the machinery gives is extremely comforting and enlightening to people, making it much easier to handle situations that come up. Most of us do not really study the root causes or the reasons why there are such things as karma and reincarnation. We accept reincarnation as a cyclical process connected to the law of cause and effect, and we leave it at that. This simple acceptance satisfies our need to explain our experience of justice and injustice.

Many people, in fact most Theosophists, find it satisfying to try to practice compassion and all of the spiritual principles that we feel are so important in our lives and to live according to natural law without bothering about theories. On the other hand, HPB said (and I think she is right about this) that without the study of metaphysics one can never know or really understand esotericism. One can never really appreciate the inner principles or the inner workings. One can never see the ways in which our lives are really tied into the whole—how the cosmos conspires to produce us and our place in the scheme of things.

2. What Is Real?

Esoteric science is really an understanding of what lies behind the phenomena. It is a study of the root causes of our behavior, rather than only the immediate causes, and of our real self. But what is the real self? We say the real self is the spiritual self. But what do we mean by that?

Unfortunately there has been a tendency in the past (not so much now, I think) in many spiritual systems to denigrate physical life. In fact, there is a meditation that used to be practiced when I was young (I am not sure that it still is): "I am not my physical self, I am my spiritual self. I am not my emotional self, I am. . . ." Well, that has always offended me, quite frankly. If you are not your physical self, would you please tell me why the cosmos has gone to all this trouble to develop a physical body?

On the other hand, I find much truer the Buddhist statement that nirvana and samsara are one and the same thing. Nirvana is that noumenal reality that extends beyond all experience, beyond all knowing, beyond all understanding, and is the root or basis of the whole universe. Samsara is the fleeting experience of physical life. But they are the same thing.

Most people are reductionists. If you ask them, "What is reality, what is real?" you get two answers. You get one answer from the religionists—and from many Theosophists—who say that the spiritual world is the real world. Since the physical world is a world of change and illusion, an appearance only, it is therefore not the real world. The real world is the spiritual realm. But those who reply in that way do not define exactly what they mean by "spiritual world." It is something "up there," uncontaminated by the "Sturm und Drang" of ordinary experience.

On the other hand, you get an opposite answer from scientists who say that the real world is the physical world. Everything else is imaginary, or derived, or conceptualized, or extrapolated from our physical experience. But, of course, today the physical world is becoming less and less seen as merely physical, at least by philosophically inclined scientists. Yet these two points of view are irreconcilable, are they not?

Theosophists, however, are not reductionists, nor are they dualists. Theosophists believe fundamentally that the same reality expressed in the spiritual component of the world—the idealism, the lawfulness, the beauty, the aesthetics, the true, the good, and the beautiful—is expressed in the physical world of appearance. These same principles govern what we call physical reality. They are one and the same thing.

How do we reconcile these two points of view? This is the task of Theosophical metaphysics and is gone into in great depth in *The Secret Doctrine*, overlaid with all kinds of embroidery from the science of the day, from mythology, from religion, from history, from other forms of human thought. But the kernel of *The Secret Doctrine*'s teachings is an explanation of how the world embodies the fundamental Reality seen by a spiritual or religious point of view.

Theosophy is not reductionist, nor is Theosophy dualistic. It doesn't say that the world is composed of two completely opposite realities, existing side by side, as Descartes said. He said you have mind, and you have matter. They are separate orders of reality which exist in parallel, simultaneously. The basis of Cartesian dualism is that we have to accept this separateness as ultimate in the universe. Well, Theosophy rejects that entirely. There are not two separate and equal indivisible realities. If there were, HPB couldn't posit an Absolute Unity, as she did in the "Proem" of *The Secret Doctrine*. Her first fundamental proposition in that "Proem" postulates

An Omnipresent, Eternal, Boundless, and Immutable PRINCIPLE on which all speculation is impossible, since it transcends the power of human conception and could only be dwarfed by any human expression or similitude. It is beyond the range and reach of thought—in the words of Mandukya [Upanishad], "unthinkable and unspeakable." [1: 14]

If you ask any Theosophist what they think is the most fundamental doctrine of Theosophy, I would say that 90 percent of them would answer "oneness" or "wholeness"—the unity of life and experience. Don't you think that is one thing that Theosophists would agree on, that we believe in the oneness of all life? But where does that oneness come from, and how does it become the diversity we perceive everywhere? The uniqueness and the diversity are both products of this fundamental oneness.

3. Same and Different

In the physical world, no two things are identical. No two leaves are absolutely alike, no two crystals, no two animals. Not even identical twins are absolutely the same; even with a common genetic heritage, no two things are the same. What does this mean? It means that uniqueness and oneness exist together. This phenomenon is completely at home in the Theosophical context, because we know that each one of us is an individual. We know our oneness. We know that we "are." We may not know *what* we are or *who* we are, but we know we "are." We have a sense of our own being. We also know that everybody else "is" and that we are not the same as anybody else.

What does this recognition of individuality mean? We tend to look at people in terms of populations, in terms of statistics. In other words, we have fifteen or twenty people here, so we add ourselves together. Does this mean we have twenty times as much human being in this room than if we just had one person? Are we twenty times more people? We look at human beings statistically instead of looking at them as individuals. But if you look from the Theosophical point of view, instead of being one-plus-one-plus-one, we have one-times-one-times-one.

Each of us is a whole person, and when you look at us in this way, you understand that no matter how many millions or even billions of people there are in the world, they all "multiply" into one, which is the human person. We are still unique and yet we are one—we are part of the greater unity. This may seem like a trivial exercise, but it involves a shift in thinking.

Because we tend to look at things statistically, we view crime in terms of being "up or down" or "how many are committing crimes." Yet every crime is committed by one individual who does it for a particular reason which is unique. There may be causes of crime, and the causes may be shared, but each individual human action is a unique event. If we look at human beings in this way, we begin to have a greater understanding. I think that science is coming around to this. I think medicine at last is also coming around to treating the whole individual rather than just the symptoms of the disease.

From the Theosophical point of view, each one of us is a divine statement in which the whole of evolution, the whole of the universe, presents itself on this particular samsaric level. We are in the crucible of life, if you like. We are nailed to the cross of matter. It is here that we have to fulfill our destiny. We have to understand the meaning of our own experience and how it relates not only to what we are, but to what we have been, and what we will be, and the process we are involved in.

4. The Will to Be

We are all involved in an ongoing process of life. We gather up our experience from the past. It is present in us as we act in the "now," while we sow the seeds, the potentialities of our future. In classic Theosophical literature "will" means "will to be," not a will to dominance over anybody. It is not that second kind of will. It is the "will to be," which I call "intentionality," because it doesn't seem to be quite as loaded a word as "will."

There are various kinds of intentionality within us—the intent to accomplish something in our lives, the intent to have a profession, the intent to be successful, the intent to have loving human relations. All of these things are part of our intent. But beneath those, we have a much deeper intent. We have a wordless intent that I think we can link to the purposefulness of our own immediate action. How we behave, our own behavior, is related to this deeper intent of our soul.

The pilgrim who embarked eons ago on what *The Secret Doctrine* calls the "cycle of necessity" has made an intentional commitment to this pilgrimage. And having made that commitment, we are carried through the long cycles of our history. Our evolutionary intent, until the next great transcendence is reached, is the commitment to our individual freedom from the bonds of desire and reactive behavior as a human being. The next big commitment is what is known in Buddhism as the Bodhisattva vow—the commitment not to work only for one's own freedom, but to renounce one's personal freedom for the sake of the whole of humanity. One will not seek freedom from this pilgrimage until all others are also free.

5. Cycles in Time

There really are stages, in a sense, of our commitment. The first is made at the very beginning. This is where I have to start talking about the pilgrim and who the pilgrim is. The foundation for it all, both the pilgrim and the pilgrimage, is given in the three fundamental propositions we are discussing. The second proposition of *The Secret Doctrine* affirms

The Eternity of the Universe *in toto* as a boundless plane; periodically "the playground of numberless Universes incessantly manifesting and disappearing," called "the manifesting stars," and the "sparks of Eternity." "The Eternity of the Pilgrim" is like a wink of the Eye of Self-Existence (Book of Dzyan). "The appearance and disappearance of Worlds is like a regular tidal ebb of flux and reflux." [1: 16–7]

Of course scientifically there is no way of proving any of these fundamental propositions. You can't prove them. But if you take them as hypotheses or postulates, then you understand how everything that we observe is in some way a fulfillment of them.

The second proposition talks about the emergence of time and the ongoing process that we are involved in. We know from science, as well as from our own personal observation, that time is unidirectional. In spite of the fact that science or science fiction talks a lot about time reversal and going backward in time machines, the only way that can work is if you think of time as moving in a circular way, so you have the whole universe and everything in it within a boundless circle. We know from Einstein that this, in theory, is so.

Space is curved, like the surface of a sphere. The sphere moves with the arrow of time and then becomes a spiral. The sphere keeps moving and unfolds as a cycle. So obviously, you have a cycle appearing in which there seem to be both an upward arc and a downward arc.

From the point of view of the one who perceives or who is involved in it, part of the arc seems to be downward. But that sense of direction is relative. A similar relative motion in astrology is called retrograde movement. A retrograde planet looks as though it is going backward. It is not really going backward, it only appears to be doing so. Similarly, if one is caught on the downward arc, one perceives it as a retrograde movement.

So this principle—the sphere combined with the arrow of time and the incessant movement that is inherent in the universe itself, in which nothing is ever stable and nothing is ever the same—is innate in both science and Theosophy. The movement, the incessant change, and the instability of the world, as well as the stable process of cyclic evolution, are set forth in the second fundamental proposition of Theosophy.

6. Transcendence and Immanence

The third proposition of *The Secret Doctrine* asserts

The fundamental identity of all Souls with the Universal Over-Soul, the latter being itself an aspect of the Unknown Root; and the obligatory pilgrimage for every Soul—a spark of the former—through the Cycle of Incarnation (or "Necessity") in accordance with Cyclic and Karmic law, during the whole term. In other words, no purely spiritual Buddhi (divine Soul) can have an independent (conscious) existence before the spark which issued from the pure Essence of the Universal Sixth principle—or the OVER-SOUL—has (a) passed through every elemental form of the phenomenal world of that Manvantara, and (b) acquired individuality, first by natural impulse, and then by self-induced and self-devised efforts (checked by its Karma), thus ascending through all the degrees of intelligence, from the lowest to the highest Manas, from mineral and plant, up to the holiest archangel (Dhyani-Buddha). [1: 17]

So both the pilgrim and the pilgrimage start. The pilgrim is the spark of the divine, in unity with what HPB calls the "Over-Soul." HPB is saying that the underlying reality, which we call divine because it is thought to be not connected with and different from the phenomenal world of appearance, is in fact present everywhere. The world, the universe, is an aspect of that divine reality.

The divine reality is not removed from its creation as it is in the Judeo-Christian-Islamic tradition, in which the Creator remains always separate from the creation. Buddhism does not speculate on that. And while in Hinduism there is a pantheon of gods, they are all aspects of the divine reality. Again and again, the Upanishads, in various statements, speak of "the one without a second," "nearer than breathing, closer than hands and feet." I have always loved that particular phrase because when we talk of the divine principle as being "nearer than breathing, closer than hands and feet," we understand that it is in us and inseparable from us. It resides in our every cell and atom.

Without the divine reality to sustain it, the world would vanish like a dream. All kinds of similes have been used, such as "The world is a dream and we are both the dream and the dreamer." All such symbolic statements try to reflect the fundamental Theosophical idea that the divine reality is transcendent. HPB says that it cannot be thought about, cannot be speculated about, cannot be experienced in the ordinary way. Yet it is also immanent because it is present in the world, in every particle of the world. It is not separate from the world. I don't want to belabor this point, but it is very important that we get it established as a basis for our understanding. We see ourselves as separate beings, until we perceive ourselves as a unit, as one, over which we have really total power.

7. Latent Powers

This is a doctrine of spiritual power. Occultism has to do with power: our power to change, our power over circumstances. This is not emphasized in ordinary Theosophical thinking. But if you go into *The Secret Doctrine*, you understand that in order to create a universe, power is needed. From the astronomical point of view, our universe is born in fire and tremendous releases of energy. The Big Bang was such an incredible eruption of force that it's unmeasurable. In the same way in the Stanzas, there is the implication of a force bursting from within without in a tremendous release of power.

If we can begin to understand the nature of human beings, we find that human beings have a tremendous reserve of power; we are powerful. We see what possibilities of violence there are; the individual can be extraordinarily violent. But the individual also has the power of understanding, of exploring, of creating.

In *The Secret Doctrine* HPB makes allusions to "Seven Keys" (1: 155n, 310, 318, 322, 325). These *Seven Keys* are related to the powers that we have to understand, powers that reside within us like the powers at the physical level, our emotional powers, our intellectual powers, our intuitive, imaginative, creative powers, and our powers of will. These *Keys* are related to the powers mentioned in the third object. Occultism, which is distinct from mystical insight, is what *The Secret Doctrine* is about. Occultism is related to the ability of human beings to use these keys to comprehend.

I think we are afraid of the word "power" because power itself is so misused. Therefore we think of it as being like an atomic bomb, something very dangerous that we are not able to handle. But if you take control of your own life, power must never be exercised against anybody else. Power is something we have to unlock and use in terms of our own life. If we try to use power to control and manipulate other people, disaster is the consequence. Because what we are doing is infringing upon their power and their right to use their own power.

Power is the potential to do something, and potential is unused power. When Theosophists talk about the powers latent in humanity, they mean everyone has these capacities. Everyone has abilities and powers because they are part of the human condition. We have developed these powers during the pilgrimage over a long, long evolutionary history. When we are inclined to denigrate ourselves, to belittle ourselves, we say, "Oh, I am not much good." We don't give proper credence or recognition or respect or admiration to what we have done, and what has been achieved by our arriving at this point in time: what and where we are with our faculties of speech and all our motor skills well developed.

According to *The Secret Doctrine*, ordinary evolutionary theory looks at life in a much more mechanical way. Life had to develop with blood, sweat, and tears because the universe did not spring fully developed, like Minerva from the brow of Zeus, perfectly articulated as it is now. It had to be constructed laboriously from the very beginning. When we look into the past, when we look into space at the stars and we see worlds as our own world was millions and millions of years ago, we begin to understand what a job it was to control that seemingly chaotic energy—to make it fecund and applicable and useful; to make it grow and change and develop; and to produce the miracle which is nature with its enormous diversity and complexity. Evolution had to develop the exquisite responsiveness of every particular creature to its environment and its ingenuity and creativity in developing its own responses to make the most of that environment.

I love to read *Natural History Magazine* because it is full of little accounts about how bugs manage to achieve an effective response to their environment. For example, leaves manage to resist the onslaught of worms by secreting things that don't taste good, and then the bugs do something to make the leaves taste better! The minutiae of things going on around us are extraordinary. It is so beautiful, what is going on at this microscopic level. What comes forth from a single cell is mind-boggling, isn't it? The thing that interests me so much is that *The Secret Doctrine* has all that in the first stanzas. It is presented in poetic language, but it is really saying the same thing.

8. Inwardness and Outwardness

I would like to say one more thing about the question of the dualism, the fundamental dualism that I mentioned earlier, on which people really get hung up. In *The Mahatma Letters* (chronological ed. letter 111, 3d ed. letter 59), the Master says "Pythagoras had a reason for never using the finite, useless figure—2, and for altogether discarding it." From the Theosophical point of view, we are confronted, as the Upanishads say, with the "pairs of opposites."

Night and day, male and female, up and down, in and out—
everything has its opposite.

We are hung up on Cartesian dualism, which states that
mind and matter are entirely separate realities. We know
that they act upon each other, but still they are different.
The materialist discounts consciousness and says it is just
a by-product of the brain. Science says the brain does certain things, and therefore we can think. People of religion
say we are a soul and we have a body, but our ultimate
destiny is to cast the body from us and have our soul free
in heaven. So, although we may give lip service to the fact
that these two areas of reality are unalterably linked together, we study them separately.

In point of fact, *The Secret Doctrine* says that dualism
is an illusion. There are not two separate realities: they are
both aspects of one reality. They are polar aspects of the
same individual reality. The third stanza says, "The Mother
swells, expanding from within without." It seems to me
those two words, "within without," are the clue to the creative power of the universe. In other words, there is a big
change, from the complete homogeneity and unity in which
nothing is going on, to this sudden "withinness" and "with-
outness." Suddenly, there is this difference of experience,
you might say, or of condition, in which it is appropriate to
speak of "within" and "without." But when we talk about
"within" and "without," we are talking about the same
thing, are we not? A single entity has an inwardness and
it has an outwardness.

I have always loved the biologist Adolph Portman because he made a very close study of living things in which

he talked about "inwardness" and "outwardness" as aspects of every living organism. In other words, each organism has an aspect you can call "consciousness" or "life," and it has an aspect you can call "organism" or "form." This is how all systems are organized, and they are all interrelated. Every system in a sense has a conscious function of its own which is fulfilled beautifully and exquisitely in terms of its relationship to all the other systems. Portman says you cannot separate the two because these functions have consequences that enhance the total life of the organism. Each organism has a consciousness of its own. It has a direction of its own. It has a purpose. All these things can be inferred from observable behavior.

As I said earlier, I like to use the words "inwardness" and "outwardness" (particularly since HPB uses the terms "within" and "without") rather than saying "consciousness and form" or "spirit and matter" although the latter are terms which are used throughout *The Secret Doctrine* and in other literature. When you talk of "spirit and matter," it is very difficult to see the implications of one to the other. They seem like two different orders of existence. But if you talk about "inwardness and outwardness," then you know these are two aspects of the same unity.

It seems to me that what happened at the time of the "Big Bang" (when "the Mother swells, expanding from within without") was a sudden shift of condition, a change of state, if you like. It is possible then to perceive an inwardness and an outwardness in the same unbroken unity. Each only exists in terms of the other. There is no separateness. The within exists only in terms of the without, and the without exists only in terms of the within. HPB also uses the terms "subjectivity" and "objectivity," which are similar. There is a subjectivity and an objectivity—but of what? They refer to consciousness or awareness, when it begins to perceive the difference between aspects of itself.

9. One Becomes Three

The next important concept is that there must be a relationship between inwardness and outwardness, between within and without. There is no within apart from a without, and vice versa. There is a relationship between the two which is energetic and implies movement. It implies looking at the within as conscious, becoming aware of the without, as well as the without responding to the within. Therefore, as soon as you set up these two polar aspects of the One, you get a third aspect: the interaction or relationship, which exists immediately.

In fact, there is no possibility of having the two polarities without having the interaction between them. This is why the Mahatma says in the letters that 2 is a useless number because "ONE can, when manifesting, become only 3." That is fundamental, and therein lies the principle of dynamism: ongoing power and energy. All things exist because of this interaction. So it is this interaction which is the key to the whole process. Of course, this relationship is intangible. It is forceful, but you can't grab it. It is not a thing. In *The Secret Doctrine*, it is called "fohat."

What is that interaction we call "fohat"? I am not going to belabor the point now, but it has to do with power, with energy, with force, with dynamism, with change, with movement. The cyclic movement that HPB talks about is tied up with these interactions, which are in the nature of an ongoing process. Because the within perceives the without and the without responds to the within, both are changed. Both are different for having perceived the other. This is the beginning of an ongoing process. This interaction exists at every level, and it is of the nature of prana or eros because it is essentially a unitive power. It unites the "within without." Therefore, you will find in *The Secret Doctrine*, if you trace it through, that fohat is of the nature of love or eros or agape.

At every level the mind can be thought of as a power. It unites the knower and the known. It reaches out and unites us with one another by the power of thought. We reach out to other people's ideas. We reach out and unite ourselves with what we are looking at and observing. It is a unitive power. People don't think of it in that way, but it is a power of uniting the "knower" and the "known." It is the power of love, the power of intuition, the power of understanding and feeling at one with things, of being able to unite yourself with them. The power of love on the emotional level, we appreciate very well. The power of love at the physical level is sexuality, which is creative power. HPB says in *The Secret Doctrine* that fohat is an intelligent power, the power that develops, unfolds if you like, from that first interaction between the within and the without, the inwardness and the outwardness.

10. The One Becomes the Many

Now, we come to a very critical thing about the One. I go back to where I said we are "one-times-one-times-one" and not "one-plus-one-plus-one." HPB says in the third fundamental proposition, that every soul is one with the "Universal Over-Soul." What is meant by this is that, even at that level, there is the potential of individuality. When you have a universal sea of beings, there is no differentiation of any kind and nothing happens. In order to create a universe, you have to have particularity and specificity. This means you are going to create a lot of things.

The potential for development of the atoms, particles, etc., which are required to create a universe, requires the development of a multiplicity of cells, all of which are of the same essence. This is the doctrine of the monad in *The Secret Doctrine*. The monad is the essential principle. HPB says, for example:

"Pilgrim" is the appellation given to our *Monad* (the two in one) during its cycle of incarnations. It is the only immortal and eternal principle in us, being an indivisible part of the integral whole—the Universal Spirit, from which it emanates, and into which it is absorbed at the end of the cycle. [1: 16 fn]

However difficult it may be for us to visualize or intellectualize it, each individual "spark" hangs from the same flame. That metaphor is used in stanza 7: "The spark hangs from the flame by the finest thread of Fohat." The energy that develops between the two polar aspects, the polarity that arises in the One, creates the monad, which is also called "the two in one."

The monad exists essentially on what you might call the noumenal level (I use Kant's words "noumenal" and "phenomenal"). It seems to me that it is easier from our point of view to understand that within the ongoing process there exists a phenomenal world which is caught up in this cycle of necessity and of pilgrimage. Once having started, you can't stop it. Once it's begun, it is self-generating and it must go through births, maturities, senescences, deaths, and regenerations. Everything must go through this cycle, whether it is a universe, a solar system, or a cycle of seasons.

This process, once it has begun, cannot stop. So, once the starting bell sounds, or there is the initial "Big Bang," the rest is inevitable. This does not mean that the universe is deterministically limited, however. Because it is a process from "within without," an infinite possibility of creative inputs exists at every level. Because the divine principle is an active one, a different turn could be taken at every point.

11. Developing the Human Condition

I don't think we can avoid what we call the "human condition." HPB said that everything in nature tends to become human. She said that—whether beginning as a stone, a plant, or a bird—all things in nature tend to become human. This isn't just anthropomorphism. What this means is that nature has to come to a point of self-conscious determination in order to fulfill its own purpose. And its purpose is to develop these powers—to develop ever more awareness, ever more information, ever more sensitivity to the environment, ever more understanding.

In order to develop those powers, it is inevitable that we come to the stage of self-consciousness. If we look at nature, we see this self-consciousness and its relationship with the environment on many levels. We see the ingenuity with which small animals overcome the obstacles in their own environment: they must have a degree of perception of the "self" and of the "other."

If I am a little chipmunk and I want to make a burrow that is going to take care of my children and take care of me through the winter, I've got to watch out for dangers—for weasels and hawks and owls. At the same time, I need to be near water. I am going to look around and find the best possible place to put my burrow. Doesn't that require some "thought" or intentionality? From the point of view of Theosophy, it is the development of the sense of self. We are not trying to define what self is, but rather get a sense of the inwardness and the outwardness.

Within us is an element of understanding, creativity, and power that can change our environment and thereby change us. Even the animal changes itself by developing certain behavioral traits in response to accomplishing what it needs to accomplish. Evolution has been called a learning process, which is a very Theosophical point of view. Evolution is a learning process in which the organism learns more about the world and thereby also learns more about itself.

On the prehuman level, the monad is not consciously learning, not intellectualizing. Animals do not theorize. They do not have theoretical knowledge, but immediate knowledge that is applicable and usable information. They use it, and they use it immediately and recognize its authenticity and its validity. They don't reflect on it.

The aspect of the mind that reflects is something only human beings have. The ability to sit back and say, "I am myself, and this is other," is a human characteristic. But according to *The Secret Doctrine*, it is derived from the Self. That Self is not the little self you and I are consciously aware of, but is a principle of Selfhood which makes possible the evolution of form and which is consonant with the deep intentionality of that divine principle which is unarticulated at the beginning, but is the impulse toward generation.

12. Logos and Monad

A lot of Theosophical literature talks about the three aspects of the logos (which is a term for the collective wisdom or intelligence within the universe) as Will, Wisdom, and Activity. But they are three misleading words. Activity really means the ability to act, the ability to create the power to externalize what is inside and thereby to create a world. Wisdom is the deep insight that comes from the very nature of what the monad is. Will is the intentionality *to be*, the drive actually to be in the world, rather than just a state of latent "be-ness."

Those three aspects reflect inwardness, outwardness, and the relationship between the two. Activity is the dynamic principle that relates the within to the without. Will or intentionality is the inwardness, the Selfhood. And Wisdom is our ability to perceive the world and to create the world in accordance with underlying principles.

The monad is said to be dual. We talk of the reawakening of the universe and "the emergence of the 'Monads' from their state of absorption within the ONE . . . the term Monad being one which may apply equally to the vastest Solar System or the tiniest atom" (1: 21). In other words, the term "monad" is used not only for individual sparks, but also for the universe as a whole.

We should understand that within everything there is an indestructible, indivisible, essential point, which is the One representing itself in everything else. *The Secret Doctrine* (1: 120) calls it "one Flame . . . [with] countless undetached sparks shining in it." HPB goes on to say that "the one fundamental law in Occult Science" is "the radical unity of the ultimate essence of each constituent part of compounds in Nature—from Star to mineral Atom, from the highest Dhyan Chohan to the smallest infusoria [microscopic lives]."

The Theosophical doctrine about the beginning of things is therefore not creation but emanation. When you say "creation," it seems to imply that the creator is separate from the creation. When you say "emanation," you understand that what emanates ("the ever-flowing fountain, the source of life and being") is continually present. The source is there at all times. So this is a very different concept of the world.

In *The Secret Doctrine*, HPB often uses the term "Parabrahm," which is taken out of the Hindu pantheon, the Upanishadic literature. Parabrahm is "that which is higher than Brahma." Brahma is considered the creative aspect of the universe, Vishnu is the preserver, and Shiva is the destroyer. These are the three aspects of the cyclic process. But Parabrahm lies beyond Brahma, beyond the creator, and is the substratum.

The spark within each individual monad, within each individual pilgrim, is identified as atma, which HPB says is identical with the universal spirit. Again, this is a term used in Indian literature, where it is said that atma and brahman are one and the same. It would be better to say that atma and Parabrahm are one and the same, and that Parabrahm's reflection in human beings is known as atma. HPB says in *The Secret Doctrine* (1: 571):

Atma (our seventh principle) being identical with the universal Spirit, and man being one with it in his essence, what is then the Monad proper? It is that homogeneous spark which radiates in millions of rays from the primeval "Seven" . . . It is *the* EMANATING *spark from the* UNCREATED *Ray*—a mystery.

It is a mystery. We can't possibly conceive of what it might be. HPB goes on to identify the One unknown with Parabrahm, which emits a bright ray from its darkness, and that is the logos, the supreme Buddha, the unmanifest Lord of all Mysteries. In other words, what HPB is saying is that at that level, there is no differentiation: Atma is One with the universe.

So how does atma become that principle within us which is the "self," which we call the "monad," the reflection of atma in the phenomenal world? In the beginning there are just clouds of fire, but it has to have a vesture. It has to draw around itself some degree of objectivity: a within and a without. It has to have a without in order to express itself. The without of atma is called buddhi or insight, and represents the first level below the spiritual level in the phenomenal world. These levels are the first and second of the planes in nature.

13. Three and Seven

HPB insisted that the planes or levels of existence are sevenfold, although subject to infinite subdivision. She had a big fight with Subba Row in the early days of the Theosophical Society because he followed an Indian four-level system corresponding generally to our terms spirit, soul, psyche, and body. HPB insisted instead upon the sevenfold scheme. One might use a categorization which lumps them together in different ways, but there are still seven levels. (Numerical or mathematical keys are one way of understanding symbolic systems and the way the universe is put together, so they are important.)

To return to the comment by the Mahatma that one can become only three, while we may talk about "one" and "three," really there is inwardness, outwardness, and their relationship to each other. That is the first trinity, and it appears throughout Theosophical literature. Most religious literature is fundamentally based on a trinity. It may be specified in different ways, but is still a trinity.

If you extrapolate from that trinity, it unfolds by developing into seven. The unfolding from three to seven is difficult to understand if you think of "one," "two," "three," and then the "quaternary." But if you name A, B, and C as the first trinity, then you have combinations of these: AB, AC, BC, and ABC; and they make seven in all. There are seven fundamental combinations of any three primary aspects, and that is the seven-fold system that *The Secret Doctrine* uses.

So the monad is the spark of the divine. HPB says in many places that the monad never was, or will be, of this world. She writes in *The Secret Doctrine* (1: 179):

It may be wrong on strictly metaphysical lines to call Atma-Buddhi a MONAD, since in the materialistic view it is dual and therefore compound. But as Matter is Spirit, and *vice-versa* [that is, inwardness and outwardness are two aspects of the same thing]; and since the Universe and the Deity which informs it are unthinkable apart from each other; so in the case of Atma-Buddhi.

That is a pretty straightforward statement from *The Secret Doctrine*. The atma part is the inwardness, and the Buddhi part is the outwardness. Their relationship creates the possibility of inwardness expressing itself outwardly, doing something or "being," and together they are therefore called a monad. If the parts were separated and the atma lost its buddhic vesture, it would vanish. It would go back into the universal flame. It would have no possibility of existence. HPB says elsewhere that the atma is blind, deaf, dumb, and incapable of acting in the world of existence without this vesture, this subtle but still material body of buddhi, which is the ability or apparatus by which it can relate itself to other things.

The monad is the basis of everything, not just the human being. We need roughly to identify what the monad is, talk about its pilgrimage up to the point of individualization, and then go on with what it means to talk about the human monad, the human self. Atma-buddhi is the foundation of everything.

There have been misunderstandings about the monad I think, based on perfectly legitimate concepts, but oversimplified in a way that cut out everything that was difficult to think about, all the paradoxes, all the ambiguities, to make a nice straightforward system. Well, that's really throwing the baby out with the bath water and getting down and worshipping the empty tub. Because what you've got left is really the husk, a mechanical system, just teaching karma and reincarnation, and if you were bad in your last life then you were going to get it in the next life. If that isn't an oversimplification, I'd like to know what is.

One simplification was of the sevenfold schema which HPB has in *The Secret Doctrine*. It starts with atma and then buddhi as a vesture of atma, and then higher and lower manas—the principle manas and the vesture of manas, which is kama-manas, linked emotion and mind, because we know we cannot separate thinking and feeling; we think a thing and we feel it. And then life, prana, the vital principle which makes us alive and functions through the etheric body or linga sharira. And then the physical body, which she said is the vehicle of all the rest.

The Secret Doctrine shows that we have a series of principles and vestures. Atma is the self in a human being, and its vesture is buddhi—intuition, creativity, the ability of the self to understand, reach out to, intuit, and react to the world. Then manas is an intelligence which is the logos principle. And the vehicle of that, the vesture of manas, is called kama-manas, our thinking and our feeling. Our thinking and feeling are but a simulacrum of mind itself, divine intelligence, which understands everything.

14. High and Low

In Buddhism, the link between manas and buddhi is called prajna, which is wisdom. It is an intuitive insight into the workings of things, which illumines the mind and makes it possible for the mind to perceive wholes, to make links, and to extrapolate from experience. The dialectical mind, on the other hand, examines, analyzes, compares, makes statistics, and so on. These two are called higher and lower mind, but I've never liked "higher" and "lower" because, if you have a "high-erarchy," you've got to be careful for then you have a "low-erarchy" too. There is no above and below, there's really only within and without.

We all make value judgments. What we have to understand is that all things in the universe, including para-

sites and other things we don't care for, are miraculous creations of the universe itself. They are the development of
the logos, the divine mind or divine intelligence, which
works itself out in infinitely creative ways to produce a universe of magnificent diversity and harmonic relationships.
The universe is very intricate, full of meaning, full of intensity of experience, full of possibility for making any kind of
world we like. Therefore, to denigrate the process by saying
it exists only so we can have spiritual insight is absolutely
shocking, and perhaps blasphemous.

The movement between the "high" and the "low" or
the within and the without is everything, as the Taoists
have understood very well. The Tao is a path, a path that
you walk on, and reality is beneath our feet as well as over
our heads. There is no such thing as a status quo, because
the status changes from moment to moment. We may feel
we're standing still, but if we're standing still, we're really
going backwards in retrograde motion.

The Chinese philosophy of change appeals to a lot
of scientists and mathematicians because it sees change as
both spontaneous and ordered. That philosophy both is
responsive to everything that's going on right now and
also has a harmonic principle within it that sees change as
part of the orderly growth of the universe—the universal
process—and not random.

15. Control, Choice, and Dharma

A lot of people feel victimized because they feel that they are subject to random events over which they have no control. But if you understand this principle of change, then you understand you always are in control. You're not in control of what happens, but you're in control of how you respond to what happens. And that's what counts. Then you're never a victim. You may be in very difficult circumstances, but you yourself always remain unviolated by those circumstances.

Human beings can really cope with anything, and we know that people have coped. People who have no arms have learned to play the piano with their toes. People can do anything they really want to, if they want to badly enough. We can really overcome almost anything because we have a limitless will or intentionality within us. It's limitless in its power to change us, to transform our selves if we perceive it so.

Annie Besant makes a wonderful statement defining dharma: "Dharma is becoming what you really are." Our life's purpose, our life's work, is to become what we really are. Now, we don't know what we really are, but we have an unconscious intuition that draws us onward. If we really open ourselves to that which will give us direction, it can move us in a certain direction and make us understand that this is the way to go without, however, setting a goal. Unrealizable goals are the worst things we can possibly have, if we want to achieve something. But we can have a kind of vector that points us in a direction.

I think many people at certain times in their lives have opened themselves up to such influence and made a change in direction because they have felt instinctively, intuitively, that it was the right way to go. Even if they had no idea where it was going to take them, how it was going to work, or what difficulties might be met on the road, it was nevertheless the best way. That is at the root of choice, the root of where freedom lies.

In spite of what Krishnamurti said, choiceless awareness is before you only after you have made all those choices, and they are all behind you. It is in making choices with regard to our own lives that our deepest freedom lies. You can talk about conditioning (and we are always dependent on conditioning), but the ultimate choices we make, the *real* choices we make, are not dependent on conditioning, but upon our own dharma, our own perception of what we really are.

16. Mysticism and Occultism

Essentially occultism and mysticism have the same goal. But you might say that, as there is a within and a without, mysticism is trying to find reality by seeking it within, whereas occultism is trying to find reality by seeking it without. Occultism looks into the nature of the universe to try to understand the laws and principles that govern life— how they express themselves, how they reveal themselves —to understand that reality by seeing its characteristics revealed in the world of nature. Mysticism tries to retreat within and discover that same reality by penetrating through the interior self.

Is an artist more a mystic than a scientist is? It depends on the person. In some ways, yes, but it's hard to generalize. An artist like Leonardo, for example, was intensely interested in the refinement of how everything worked. So in a way you'd have to say he was sort of an occultist; he was almost an alchemist because he was fascinated by the way the principles of nature become articulated in form.

Those who are interested in the formative side of nature, and many artists are, are on the path of occultism because the development of form is one of the creative powers of the divine mind. A lot of people think that the arupa or formless world is much higher and more spiritual than the rupa or form world.

One group of people who understood form, its mysteries, and its marvels were the Muslims. Muslim architecture embodies the golden section, the intricate geometry, all the principles; even the Platonic forms are exhibited and elaborated in Islamic architecture in a miraculous way. The Muslims understood that the form reveals the idea and makes it accessible to human beings.

The same is true in music. A musician has to use all the harmonic principles, willy nilly, whether he wants to or not. They are not something dreamt up or decided. They are there.

Art doesn't work unless it's delimited. You have to have a canvas and that canvas in some way identifies and delimits artistic expression. The way of the occultist is to discover the inner meaning of form so that form is liberating, not confining.

Form defines the spirit or the consciousness of a being. All you have to do is look at an animal and understand that the form of that animal is really expressive of its inner being. No matter whether it is an elephant, a lion, a giraffe, a mouse, or a worm, its form is really the creation of the animal in response to its environment.

Scientists say that the evolution of form is only a response to the pressures of the environment. I do not think so. I think form evolves in response to the environment, but it does so in order to free the animal more and more, to help it live in its environment more and more fully. So the way an animal moves and its relationship to the earth and the sky are intensely significant.

Therefore, form and the study of form are essential on the path of occultism, which is not just a study of magic. A study of the laws that govern form and of the principles and dynamics within form is essential on that path. On the other hand, mysticism disregards the form. Forms dissolve and disappear in the intense mystical experience of the inwardness which imbues and infuses all forms.

Mysticism and occultism are different ways of arriving at the same goal, but you can combine them. Once a person has proceeded a way on either path, there is a realization of the mystery and the beauty that lies behind it. Nothing can ever be understood entirely intellectually with the mind. You have to unite yourself with it.

You might say that artists have a foot on each path. A lot of artists today would say they are not interested in form, they are interested in freeing themselves. But you can never escape form, so they are creating other kinds of form, how successfully depends on how good they are as artists.

17. Form, Energy, Consciousness

The rules of form were established for all worlds when those worlds were laid down. It is hard to conceive of a form that does not have within it the elements that everyone recognizes in a form—curves, radiating lines, spaces, and so on. It would be very difficult to do without such elements. I mean, inadvertently one would use these elements because they are part of us, part of our own form, and therefore they would be pretty hard to escape.

The important thing is what creates forms. Are they fortuitous? No! A Theosophist would never say they are fortuitous. They are created when the worlds are laid down on ordered and orderly principles (mathematical, relational, harmonic, musical, sympathetic vibrations), and they are manifested because the primary creative energy is the basic interrelationship between the inwardness and the outwardness.

That primary energy is therefore an intelligent energy, not just a mechanical relationship. According to *The Secret Doctrine*, the name for the interactive power between the inwardness and the outwardness, subject and object, is "fohat," which is an intelligent, fiery energy. All types of energy are transformations of fohat.

Scientists today are trying to integrate the universal forces and have now managed to unify the electromagnetic force with the weak and strong nuclear forces, but gravity escapes them entirely. They haven't a clue how to get gravity into that picture. HPB said in *The Secret Doctrine* (remember she wrote this over a hundred years ago when these scientific notions had not even been thought of) that fohat is the one energy of which all other forms of energy are manifestations of various kinds. She said this energy is an intelligent not a mechanical energy, involving the relationship of consciousness to its object.

All forms of energy, no matter what they are, have a degree of consciousness, a degree of intelligence, or a degree of adaptivity to the needs of the particular form. Whether or not this will ever be proved scientifically, we don't know. What I am trying to point out is that the worlds, according to *The Secret Doctrine*, are created from "within without" or "as above, so below," not starting with a world of matter and then deriving life and intelligence from it—higher forms of life evolving out of the mud, so to speak. From the Theosophical point of view, the planes, the worlds, proceed from "within without" and the highest realms are created first.

When I say "worlds," I mean what we call the different levels of consciousness and energy. Think of a "world" as a state or condition of being in which there is a great deal of reciprocity between the inward and the outward, between consciousness and the outward environment. That's a world.

18. The Course of Evolution

When we look out at the starry universe, we have to understand that a world like ours—an earth with many diverse forms of life, plants and animals and human beings —is a very late stage of development. Some other worlds, which seem nebulous and fiery, may be going through earlier stages of development. And of course, there may be others that are now beyond their peak and are dying. As far as *The Secret Doctrine* is concerned, it has taken eons and eons of time for us to develop a planet like this with human beings of the kind we are.

The whole second volume of *The Secret Doctrine* is devoted to an account of the evolutionary scheme of our planet: how it took place, how long it took, and how it was developed. This story of rounds, races, and globes is one that is usually ignored by contemporary Theosophists. It is very difficult for us to map this story onto our own experience or onto our own science, because it does not map well. You can map it onto the symbolic histories and the allegories in the great religions, but these are not working myths in our culture. They are of some interest to historians and mythologists, but they don't seem very apropos now. Therefore, I think Theosophists, myself included, don't talk much about this subject.

But we have to understand that not only in *The Secret Doctrine*, but also in *The Mahatma Letters*, a great deal of space and time is given to this subject. When we look up "monad" in *The Mahatma Letters*, we find a great deal about the progress and the evolution of the monad through these various cycles of globes and kingdoms. One wonders why the Mahatmas put such emphasis on this subject because it is going to remain speculative for a long, long time. There is no way of connecting it with our experience.

The Secret Doctrine makes many extraordinary statements. One of these statements is that human beings appeared before the other mammals on the Earth. That is an extraordinary statement as far as scientists are concerned, because they are convinced that mammals started in the age of dinosaurs and the human species much later. When *The Secret Doctrine* talks about the human being, however, it is talking about a particular stage in evolution, a state of consciousness, a kind of being. It is not talking about some creature that walks upright and has opposing thumbs and can do certain things.

The human stage is considered critical. When we say that "man is the measure of all things," the statement is meant literally because the evolution of consciousness has critical stages. One of the most critical is the human evolution. So when *The Secret Doctrine* says that mammals could not appear until human beings had fostered their evolution, it means that the human ability to objectify and to relate to its environment as a "self" quickened the evolution of nature itself.

You know today we do nothing but think of ourselves as the spoilers of the environment, out there ruining everything. We never think from *The Secret Doctrine*'s point of view, in which human beings are, in a sense, the creators of nature because of our very awareness of the world around us.

The Secret Doctrine goes back millions of years to human beings in one form or another living on this earth, not formed like us, but as conscious entities.

I know this all sounds very extraordinary, so I don't blame you if you are skeptical that a "quickening" of the mind helped quicken evolution on Earth. We know from paleontology that evolution was extremely slow for a long period of time. Then there was an immense proliferation of organisms. According to *The Secret Doctrine*, this was due to the influence of the self-conscious mind during the "cycle of necessity."

19. Atma-Buddhi and the Monad

The "Monad," born of the nature and the very Essence of the "Seven" . . . , has to perform its septenary gyration throughout the Cycle of Being and forms, from the highest to the lowest; and then again from man to God. At the threshold of Paranirvana it reassumes its primeval Essence and becomes the Absolute once more. [1: 135]

The Sixth principle in Man (Buddhi, the Divine Soul) though a mere breath, in our conceptions, is still something material when compared with divine "Spirit" (Atma) of which it is the carrier or vehicle. Fohat, in his capacity of DIVINE LOVE *(Eros)*, the electric Power of affinity and sympathy, is shown allegorically as trying to bring the pure Spirit, the Ray inseparable from the ONE absolute, into union with the Soul, the two constituting in Man the MONAD, and in Nature the first link between the ever unconditioned and the manifested. "The first is now the second." [1: 119]

That statement refers to the same principle which governs the whole process of the development of the manifested world through the action of fohat, the principle of intelligent affinity which draws things together. This principle is essential in order to compose the world. It is a pro-creative principle entirely.

Buddhi is what you might call the first vesture of the spirit, and it is created first because the monads are created long before there is a world for them to inhabit. A lot of people think of atma as a ray. Many people think it is not of this world and is therefore unrealizable. I don't believe that is true. I think that if atma were not present in each one of us, we would be nothing.

The fact is that, in very badly disabled and damaged human beings who are not able to function at all, the connection with atma is blocked. But in everyone—even if it's a person who is violent and does all kinds of things that we consider aberrant behavior—there still is that connection. If that connection were not present, the person wouldn't be able to function at all. Of course, you can have malfunctioning persons at various levels. I mean you can have brain malfunctions, and other such blockages, but even within a very damaged vehicle something is present.

Metaphysically speaking, it is of course an absurdity to talk of the "development" of a Monad, or to say that *it* becomes "Man."... It stands to reason that a MONAD cannot either progress or develop, or even be affected by the changes of states it passes through. *It is not of this world or plane,* and may be compared only to an indestructible star of divine light and fire, thrown down on to our Earth as a plank of salvation for the personalities in which it indwells. It is for the latter to cling to it; and thus partaking of its divine nature, obtain immortality. Left to itself the Monad will cling to no one; but, like the "plank," be drifted away to another incarnation by the unresting current of evolution. [1:174 fn]

But the human must cling to its imperishable monad through the force of will or intentionality. So you see, the monad is, in a sense, nothing when it begins. It is in itself nothing and has had no experience.

The interesting thing is the implication that the monads create the world. In other words, consciousnesses develop in the worlds by living in them, by using them, by developing their material. This is what I said about the fact that we human beings by being on this earth have changed the earth radically—not only changed it by what we do to it, but changed it by what we are within ourselves. We as a species are very often harmful and violent and destructive, but we are an evolutionary force according to *The Secret Doctrine*. I don't think this is necessarily so according to science.

Human beings have been significant forces in evolution. Our planet is becoming humanized at an almost alarming rate. And now people are beginning to develop a sense of responsibility, that the world is not there for us to exploit, but for us to nurture. Human beings are custodians of nature, of our world. This idea is brand new in our culture. We are only just beginning to understand our responsibility. According to *The Secret Doctrine* this responsibility has always existed.

We have to understand that, from the Theosophical point of view, at the human stage we are far along on the evolutionary path. We have an enormous history behind us. That history is not necessarily only as human beings. If we take ourselves as a human monad, which now has developed a soul through the attachment of manas, we existed for eons before we even reached the point of individualization. This is when we really become human, because the monad has existed since the beginning of time.

20. Monad: Its Numbers and Evolution

There are all kinds of problems with this concept of the monad. HPB says, "The spiritual Monad is One, Universal, Boundless and Impartite" (1: 177), but then how do you account for the fact that we have various stages in evolution, and obviously there are some monads in advance of others? The kingdoms of nature are not all the same. They are not equally self-conscious, and they are not equally responsive.

Some human beings seem to be more in advance of others. Nobody could say that the Buddha was not far in advance of all the rest of us, isn't that so? So how do you account for that? I think we started moving through time in a cycle. Some of the monads emerged later than others in what HPB calls "evolutionary waves." So although all monads are exactly the same, some of them began on the pilgrimage earlier than others. HPB says that although the monads are countless, they are finite in number. There are not ever more and more of them. New monads are not coming into existence all the time. The door is closed.

Adam Warcup gave a lecture in which he said that people had asked him why there were so many more people in existence now than there were before. He said that he felt it was due to various lapses in recorded history, which only covers a very short period of time. I wish I were totally satisfied with that. I think it is very mysterious how this happens.

All our ordinary ideas of space and time may not apply to this problem. We cannot measure or look at this problem in terms of our usual space-time parameters because it goes beyond them. A great many other things are involved. I think time may speed up and slow down. Since Blavatsky said that the door is closed, that no more new monads are coming into the system, I assume she meant what she said. But I think there are many, many hidden factors and it is the province of occultism to discover some of those.

Scientists are beginning to penetrate that domain. For example, at the quantum level, particles appear and disappear; I think they're just stepping in and out of incarnation. Their life span is extremely brief. I think they appear and disappear because they are at the threshold between the other worlds and the physical world. Their incarnations might be an infinitesimal amount of time.

Our whole evolutionary history is alive and well in each one of us right here and now. All the forms of the mineral kingdom, all the elements, are essential to us. Unless you have those minerals present, you languish and die. All the vegetative things are also in us. The flow of blood is like the flow of sap. Respiration begins with the trees. We couldn't live without their giving off oxygen and our giving off carbon dioxide. And the animal is very present in us too.

We, in ourselves, embody not only what you might call the physical evolutionary stages, but the psychic evolutionary stages that we have gone through, as well. According to *The Secret Doctrine*, the evolution of the psychic level had to occur first, before we could even begin physical evolution. Because the physical world is dependent upon the evolution of the psychic world, it is dependent upon the inner resources of all creatures.

The monad is present and is essential in the building of the worlds of form. HPB uses the word *monad* in many ways. She uses it to refer to the whole universal process. She uses it to refer to the great angelic beings that begin to create the worlds of form. She uses it in connection with the minerals and many other things, so you begin to think everything is a monad. The following passage from *The Secret Doctrine* (1: 177–8) may make the concept of the monad a little clearer:

The spiritual Monad is One, Universal, Boundless and Impartite, whose rays, nevertheless, form what we, in our ignorance, call the "Individual Monads" of men, so the Mineral Monad . . . is also One—and from it proceed the countless physical atoms.

This is not to say that a whole mountaintop is one monad. It is not that at all. It is the monad which is developing through that form of materiality which is called the mineral kingdom. You cannot say there is one monad per Himalayan or Appalachian mountain range. That is not the way to think of it at all. We have to think of the mineral kingdom as evolving at a particular stage that a monad is overshadowing.

In other words, as the human evolutionary stage is focused in the individual, the monadic rays are here centered in the upper triad or spiritual ego. Whereas, at the mineral stage, no triad has yet been formed because the monad is not linked up yet. That only happens when you become a human being. The monad is focused at the physical atomic level in the mineral stage. That is where the monad is working, that is its field of operation.

This is why one cannot justifiably speak of the evolution of the monad through the kingdoms. It is the kingdoms that are evolving. The monad remains the impulse. A dog will never be a genius because the dog is not individualized. The monad that is present in the dog is developing all the doggie characteristics that we find so appealing and so is representative of a stage of life or "livingness." The monad is present in the kingdoms and is evolving those kingdoms. The kingdoms are evolving, not the monad. It is the presence of the monad that makes the kingdom evolve. Thus, the monadic impulse, the "will to be," creates the kingdoms and the levels of consciousness by shining in and on the appropriate kind of matter and energy: mineral/physical, vegetable/emotional, animal/psychic (kama-manas), and human/atma-buddhi-manas or spiritual triad. So you see that, before individual consciousness can evolve in the world, the worlds have to be created.

21. Involution and Evolution

The reason *The Mahatma Letters* and *The Secret Doctrine* spend so much time on the creation of the world itself, involving all these rounds and races and cycles, is to illustrate that these worlds have to be evolved first. The development of the actual physical form is an immense labor, and we don't think much about it. We think of evolution beginning from that point onward. We don't realize that it took much longer to get down to the physical level of having a mineral kingdom in which the monad could have material to do something with.

The principle of involution is a terribly important one. It is the penetration or the dropping down of the monad, involving itself more and more deeply in matter until the physical world is a possibility. In the earlier stages there really wasn't a physical world. And this is why *The Secret Doctrine* says that we do not find any remains, because early human beings inhabited the world when they weren't really physical yet. They were more like etheric creatures. They didn't have substantial bodies, but had to gradually evolve those.

The Secret Doctrine discusses the great root races, which are great epochs involving millions of years of the laying down and the gradual physicalization of the world, bringing it through the etheric and gradually solidifying it, so that the early races developed each sense, one by one. For example, the first root race developed the sense of hearing. Each race has the task of developing one of the senses.

What an immense procedure this was! Science does not recognize any of this, and I am not sure that it ever will, because there are no artifacts or paleontological remains.

The cycle has seven stages: there are three elemental kingdoms, then the mineral, the vegetable, the animal, the human, and stages beyond. When we get to the human cycle, the door is closed. There are no monads going through that whole process any more, because the process has been completed. The elemental kingdoms were laid down, the mineral kingdom was established, the other kingdoms were established, and now the wave of evolution is on the upward arc of spiritualization.

So that's where the evolutionary impulse is as yet. HPB refers to it with the kabbalistic axiom: "A stone becomes a plant; a plant, a beast; a beast, a man; a man, a spirit; and the spirit, a god" (1: 197). She also says:

The Monad or Jiva . . . is, first of all, shot down by the law of Evolution into the lowest form of matter—the mineral. After a sevenfold gyration encased in the stone (or that which will become mineral and stone in the Fourth Round), it creeps out of it, say, as a lichen. Passing thence, through all the forms of vegetable matter, into what is termed animal matter, it has now reached the point in which it has become the germ, so to speak, of the animal, that will become the physical man. All this, up to the Third Round, is formless, as matter, and senseless, as consciousness. For the Monad or Jiva *per se* cannot be even called spirit: it is a ray, a breath of the ABSOLUTE, or the Absoluteness rather, and the Absolute Homogeneity, having no relations with the conditioned and relative finiteness, is unconscious on our plane. Therefore, besides the material which will be needed for its future human form, the monad requires (*a*) a spiritual model, or prototype, for that material to shape itself into; and (b) an intelligent consciousness to guide its evolution and progress, neither of which is possessed by the homogeneous monad, or by senseless though living matter. [1: 246–7]

The term "jiva" when used with "monad" means the monad which is living, alive. The word "jiva" means "life." So "monad" and "jiva" used together refer to the monad associated with the living being. When the monad, which is changeless and immortal, is called "jiva," that is, "life," which is vital change in growing and learning all the time, the two contradictory descriptions must be meant to indicate the different conditions or changes of state which the monad experiences, not changes of being in itself. It is somewhat like the particle-wave relationship at the quantum level. The conditions can be seen as complementary, not contradictory, like duration and time.

So when the monad is talked of as jiva, it means that the monad is in that stage or condition in life in which it is associating with a living being. Sometimes when you read *The Secret Doctrine*, you think, "What does it mean when it says the monad is like a ray, and never of this world, and then it's called jiva?" It's as though these things try deliberately to confuse us.

22. The Mineral and Other Monads

The Secret Doctrine (1: 178) says this about the monad and minerals:

It would be very misleading to imagine a Monad as a separate Entity trailing its slow way in a distinct path through the lower Kingdoms, and . . . flowering into a human being; in short, that the Monad of a Humboldt dates back to the Monad of an atom of hornblende.

That's what unfortunately seems to be implied in some of the literature that has tried to simplify the idea. The passage goes on:

Instead of saying a "Mineral Monad," the more correct phraseology . . . would of course have been to call it "the Monad manifesting in that form of Prakriti [or materiality] called the Mineral Kingdom." The atom . . . is not a particle of something, animated by a psychic something, destined after aeons to blossom as a man. But it is a concrete manifestation of the Universal Energy which itself has not yet become individualized; a sequential manifestation of the one Universal Monas. The ocean (of matter) does not divide into its potential and constituent drops until the sweep of the life-impulse reaches the evolutionary stage of man-birth.

All of nature is One. Nature is unified in a way that human beings never can be because we are self-conscious. We are aware of ourselves as individual separate beings. I am different from you. You are different from me. I look at you and you look at me, and we have an interaction, but we are not the same. This is fundamental to the human condition, this anomaly, this sense of reaching out to everyone, needing other people, and yet having a sense of "I am myself and I am unique." This takes place at the level of the ahamkara, the "I-making." HPB continues:

The tendency towards segregation into individual Monads is gradual, and in the higher animals comes almost to the point.

The higher animals almost become self-conscious. That doesn't mean that they are individuals, but you know how animals want you to do things for them. I have a dog, and it comes and says, "I want my biscuits! Give them to me! Now! I want the biscuit. Why don't you give it to me now!" That kind of sense of self is developed in animals, but it is not yet anything really equivalent to the human sense of self-consciousness or self-awareness. Next HPB says:

The Peripatetics applied the word Monas to the whole Kosmos, . . . and the Occultists . . . distinguish the progressive stages of the evolution of the concrete from the abstract by terms of which the "Mineral, Vegetable, Animal, (etc.), Monad" are examples.

But the mineral monad is still One. It hasn't separated itself into a whole flock of mineral monads. It is one monad.

The term [mineral or vegetable or animal monad] merely means that the tidal wave of spiritual evolution is passing through that arc of its circuit. The "Monadic Essence" [which is diffused entirely and not associated with any particular form] begins to imperceptibly differentiate towards individual consciousness in the Vegetable Kingdom. As the Monads are uncompounded things, . . . it is the spiritual essence which vivifies them in their degrees of differentiation, which properly constitutes the Monad—not the atomic aggregation, which is only the vehicle and the substance through which thrill the lower and the higher degrees of intelligence. [1: 178–9]

HPB wrote much of what I have been quoting about the mineral monad in reply to some questions raised by A. P. Sinnett's *Esoteric Buddhism* (CW 5: 171–5). In particular, in that reply she says: "In short, the mineral monad is *one*—the higher animal and human monads are countless" (172). She also says in *The Secret Doctrine* that there were no mammals until human beings appeared on earth. Some people think of animals as being our ancestors, and in one way they are because the monad has passed through the arc of animal evolution. In other ways the animals are our children, because we have established the environment in which they can live and learn. So from the point of view of *The Secret Doctrine*, animals are our responsibility. This is a very different point of view.

There are seven kingdoms. The first group comprises three degrees of elementals, or nascent centres of forces . . . from full unconsciousness to semi-perception; the second or higher group embraces the kingdoms from vegetable to man; the mineral kingdom thus forming the central or turning point in the degrees of the "Monadic Essence," considered as an evoluting energy. Three stages (sub-physical) on the elemental side; the mineral kingdom; three stages on the objective physical side—these are the (first or preliminary) seven links of the evolutionary chain. [1: 176]

Blavatsky talks about "Monadic Essence." Monadic essence is very mysterious. It's puzzled me for a long time—but I was reading a book by James Gleick called *Genius: The Life and Science of Richard Feynman*. It says that quantum mechanics views a particle not as a particle but as a smudge, a traveling cloud of probabilities, which is like a wave in that its essence is spread out. Might monadic essence be somewhat analogous, in that it is wave-like, not particulate or well-defined but spread out within its own field or domain? The monad in the human stage undergoes a change of state and becomes particle-like or well-defined. Perhaps even in the animal stage it becomes more particle-like or has longer periods of being like a particle.

Or perhaps it is like the process of crystallization. When the mother liquid gets to the point of crystallization, the whole solution crystallizes in an instant. That change, flashing through, gives you the feeling of what's going on. A particular crystalline form has been determined out of the liquid.

The Secret Doctrine, it seems to me, clearly defines the range of the mineral kingdom. Quantum mechanics would give the electron a definite point-like position which makes it possible for electrons and atoms to maintain their position and stability, thus allowing for durable form and structure. According to *The Secret Doctrine* the aim of evolution in the mineral phase is earth-building. That is its goal and purpose. The distribution of the charged electrons creates an energy force which holds the nucleus of an atom in place. Force has both magnitude and a direction or vector quality. Energy has magnitude only. It is directionless.

Thus the monadic impulse, the "will to be," creates the kingdoms and the levels of consciousness by "shining in" and on the appropriate stage of matter and energy.

Those unable to seize the difference between the monad—the Universal Unit—and the *Monads* or the manifested Unity, as also between the ever-hidden and the revealed LOGOS or the *Word*, ought never to meddle in philosophy, let alone the Esoteric Sciences. [1: 614]

She is saying, if you can't see the difference, leave it alone! Of this difference between the underlying wholeness, the "Universal Unity," and the "manifested Unity," which manifests itself in diverse ways, she says:

What it really meant was the triune co-equal Nature of the first differentiated Substance, or the *con-substantiality* of the (manifested) Spirit, matter and the Universe—their "Son," who proceeds from the Point (the real, esoteric LOGOS) or the Pythagorean MONAD. . . . Those who have . . . understood . . . will see clearly the line we draw between the *absolutely Ideal* Universe and the invisible though manifested Kosmos. [1: 614]

HPB says you have to understand the difference between the reality—the invisible, absolutely ideal universe —and the process that is going on. Even though that universe is invisible to us, it is still manifested:

Our Gods and Monads are not the Elements of *extension* itself [the complex machinery, you might say—everything that is going on], but only those of the invisible reality which is the basis of the manifested Kosmos. . . . The Circle and the Point, which latter retires into and merges with the former, after having emanated the first three points and connected them with lines, thus form the first *noumenal* basis of the Second Triangle in the Manifested World. [1: 614]

She also says:

The Monad or Jiva . . . is, first of all, shot down by the law of Evolution into the lowest form of matter—the mineral. [1: 246]

The three stages preceding it are elemental or subphysical and are permeated by the monadic essence, which implies a complete lack of differentiation, if the monads can be said to undergo differentiation in their later development.

The mineral "monad" is not an individuality latent, but an all-pervading Force which has for its present vehicle matter in its lowest and most concrete terrestrial state. [CW 5: 175]

So we mustn't think of a monad as being imprisoned in a mountain or something like that. We must think of the mountain as an expression of the monad in that particular kingdom of life. It is a subtle difference. HPB continues:

In man the monad is fully developed, potential, and either passive or absolutely active, according to its vehicle, the five lower and more physical human principles.

The human monads are each individual, though essentially the same. But according to the condition in which they themselves exist, they differ. The monad of Einstein and of a man on death row are equally pure. You cannot sully a monad. At that level, they are uncontaminated by violence or any of the divisive emotions. But because it is associated with a vehicle through which it cannot shine, it doesn't have much influence. It's there and is not affected by the violence of the life, but it is ineffective in that it cannot make the contact. HPB concludes her discussion of the mineral monad by looking in the opposite direction from the human monad:

In the Deva kingdom it [the monad] is fully liberated and in its highest state—but one degree lower than the ONE Universal Life.

Blavatsky approvingly quotes a lecture on Leibnitz as proposing that elementary particles

are *centres of force,* or rather "spiritual beings whose very nature is to act," for the elementary particles are not acting mechanically, but from an *internal* principle. . . . Leibnitz's monads . . . "differ from atoms in the following particulars. . . . Atoms are not distinguished from each other, they are qualitatively alike; but one monad differs from every other monad qualitatively; and every one is a peculiar world to itself." [1: 630]

Now when she says that, you wonder, because at one point she says the monads are absolutely all the same, and then she quotes someone as saying they differ qualitatively, and every one is a peculiar world to itself. Those seem like contradictions, don't they? If each monad does differ from every other, their difference is surely rooted in the second fundamental proposition, which we talked about: periodicity or the emergence of the space-time continuum. The differentiation between monads can only be due to shifts in space and time, not in the monads themselves, because they are all equal. They are different because of their circumstances, their emergence. Their evolutionary states are different. That's what the difference is.

HPB continues to quote the lecture:

These monads are representative Beings. Every monad reflects every other. Every monad is a living mirror of the Universe within its own sphere. . . . in mirroring the world, the monads are not mere passive reflective agents, but *spontaneously self-active;* they produce the images spontaneously, as the soul does a dream. [1: 631]

When Blavatsky cites the word "images," you may immediately think of the world of appearance, of maya. And then you understand that the monads are the creative agents of the world. She reiterates again and again that there would not be a world like this if it were not informed from within by these spiritual foci, which are the monads.

Thus the monads are like holograms of the universal All. They are worlds to themselves, but the degree to which these phenomenal images reflect the metaphysical truth of the noumenal reality differs according to their degree of evolutionary progress and experience. All the portions of the universe are represented by monads, but some are reflected in one monad and some in another, because they haven't gotten to the point of being universal. So that's enough about the monads within themselves, up to the point of human incarnation.

The mineral kingdom has accomplished its task. What is its task? If you consider the gunas of Indian philosophy —rajas, tamas, and sattva—the mineral kingdom has the tamasic element. That element of stability, the foundation for life upon which you can build, upon which you can be fecund and have earth and growing parts, had to be established first. The earth's crust had to be built. We know that the earth's crust moves and changes, with mountain building and shifting masses. It has its own dynamism; it has volcanism. So its task isn't finished—it's still a living entity.

But the evolutionary wave has in a sense left the mineral kingdom and passed on. The focus of evolution was entirely in the mineral kingdom at the time when the earth was molten and full of volcanism. The evolutionary focus, which HPB calls the life-wave, was focused in the mineral kingdom for eons, for many millions of years, before the earth became sufficiently stable for crust formation, mountain building, and all of that.

Then the evolutionary wave might be said to have passed from the mineral into the vegetable kingdom, although science now thinks that vegetation and other living animal organisms developed simultaneously. Vegetation requires the agency of animals like moths and butterflies, flying insects for pollination, and various things like that. Maybe insects, which we now know are millions of years old—because they're captured in amber and so on—arose simultaneously with plants. Maybe insects are just a form of vegetable life in a more mobile form? I don't think HPB talks about insects much—I wonder whether insects are related to the vegetable kingdom in some peculiar way more than other animals are.

We can't say that the mineral kingdom is finished, but new minerals are not being discovered. New minerals are not being made in volcanoes. The life-wave has passed through the mineral kingdom and is now on the upward arc, and the focus of evolutionary development is on the higher kingdoms.

23. The Monad: Source and Presence

With regard to the pilgrimage itself, the human monad and the human soul are two different things. We must differentiate between spirit and soul. I think most people apprehend that there is a great deal of difference between the spirit and the soul.

I'm not too fond of Gurdjieff, but he once made a statement which was quite startling to me. I have come to think that he's correct. He says somewhere that every human being creates his or her own soul. That is actually true because the spirit is emanated and is sui generis.

"Emanation" means that something is born out of a higher reality, but that reality is never diminished though it participates in the creation. The sun gives of itself, it shines forth, it emanates life. It's not a strict analogy because the sun uses up its substance eventually, but the spiritual reality that is behind everything is never diminished. However many universes and cosmoses are developed out of that, it itself is never diminished. It emanates.

The German title of Jean Gebser's book *Ursprung und Gegenwart* (literally "source and presence") has been translated as "the everflowing source." That translation expresses the idea. The source is always present in the flow. The spring is present in the river. There is absolute continuity, not only continuity of substance, but continuity of being. Therefore I think emanation is the Theosophical position on how the worlds are born.

We have to understand that the world and we ourselves are both durable and changeable at the same time. That is a contradiction, a paradox, just like oneness and uniqueness. At the bottom of this whole doctrine there is a paradox; we cannot think about it in our terms or impose our logic upon it. We don't like contradictions, anomalies, paradoxes. They leave us, we feel, hanging in mid air. But we have to reconcile ourselves to the fact that we live in a world full of paradoxes and contradictions. It transcends our logic, it transcends our mind.

We can never really think about these ultimate questions because the mind operates in very special and specific ways. The mind is what's needed to develop specificity. Without it we would not have specificity. That in a way is one of its functions. Its other function is to comprehend, in some way illumined by the intuition, the connections between specificity and generality.

I would like to read a number of passages to you because then you get the authentic words that HPB uses. She makes very strong statements about what a human being really is. The first passage is from volume 1, page 247:

For the Monad or Jiva *per se* cannot be even called spirit: it is a ray, a breath of the ABSOLUTE, or the Absoluteness rather, and the Absolute Homogeneity, having no relations with the conditioned and relative finiteness, is unconscious on our plane.

She keeps reiterating the unity of the Absolute and the human monad as well as the monad as it is present in the various kingdoms of the earth. Our universe of change is relative and relational, so the monad, which is not conscious of change, movement, and diversity, cannot be conscious on our level.

Therefore, besides the material which will be needed for its future human form, the monad requires (a) a spiritual model, or prototype, for that material to shape itself into; and (b) an intelligent consciousness to guide its evolution and progress, neither of which is possessed by the homogeneous monad, or by senseless though living matter. The Adam of dust requires the *Soul of Life* to be breathed into him: the two middle principles, which are the *sentient* life of the irrational animal and the Human Soul, for the former is irrational without the latter.

In other words, the soul is the monad plus manas. Everywhere in the literature atma-buddhi-manas is called the human soul. Atma-buddhi captures manas, or shall we say it the other way around—that manas, the intelligent aspect which is the logos, captures the monad?

The logos doctrine is worthy of a good deal of attention. We have to understand what we mean by the logos. The term is used very much in Christianity in the correct sense of "the word," the articulated divine intelligence—articulated, that is, related to specificity. It is what is imbued within us or shall we say we are modeled on its prototype?

In many ways, Plato was a theosophist although he talks about his archetypes as static and fixed and says that everything is then built upon them, and I don't think the Theosophical idea is that at all. In the Theosophical sense, the archetypes are living divine intelligences, even beings in the same sense that in Christianity there are powers and principalities and archangels and so on, which help in the construction of the universe.

We shouldn't anthropomorphize these divine intelligences, but in a sense they are humanlike. It is said that everything in nature is, has been, or will be human. These divine intelligences are in a sense beings that have transcended the human condition, gone way beyond, and they are getting the results of all of their experience and their understanding in developing a new universe. The making of new worlds is a continuous process.

In connection with that, I have another quotation (2: 42):

Nature (in man) must become a compound of Spirit and Matter before he becomes what he is [not "will be"]; and the Spirit latent in Matter must be awakened to life and consciousness gradually. The Monad has to pass through its mineral, vegetable and animal forms, before the Light of the Logos [that is, intelligence or divine mind—universal intelligence, not specific intelligence] is awakened in the animal man. Therefore, till then, the latter cannot be referred to as "MAN," but has to be regarded as a Monad imprisoned in ever changing forms.

And then she goes on (2: 56):

Thus physical nature, when left to herself in the creation of animal and man, is shown to have failed. She can produce the first two [that is, the mineral and the vegetable] and the lower animal kingdoms, but when it comes to the turn of man, spiritual, independent and intelligent powers are required for his creation . . . . The human Monads . . . need something higher than purely physical materials to build their personalities [that is, their lower principles] with.

24. The Human Monad

So the creation of humans, according to *The Secret Doctrine*, is an onerous process. We're inclined to think of ourselves, from certain religious perspectives, as divine creations. On the other hand, from the scientific point of view, we think of ourselves as a product of physical evolution. From *The Secret Doctrine*'s point of view, both of those processes are necessary to produce humanity. A descent of the spiritual and an ascent of the material are both needed to come to a point of fusion, whereby the antahkarana is built, which is the channel, the link between the highest and the lowest. Before a divine intelligence can make an imprint on the world, the means for its doing so must exist.

The human monad is a great mystery. For example, HPB says:

The "human" Monad, whether *immetallized* in the stone-atom, or *invegetallized* in the plant, or *inanimalized* in the animal, is still and ever a divine, hence also a HUMAN Monad. [2: 185]

She's made up a few words here, but what she seems to be saying is that the monad, even before it ever enters the human stage, is a prototypical human. This is said in many other places in *The Secret Doctrine*: Man is the measure of all things, Man is the fulcrum, Man is the focus of evolution, Man is the critical point, Man is hung on the cross of matter. These symbolical statements are not talking about human beings like you and me, who are imperfect.

We're not really human yet in one sense. We're only partly human. We have all the potentialities of becoming human, but we are using or have as yet access to only a fraction of what we really are. According to *The Secret Doctrine*, we will not really become what is meant by a human being until we use fully the powers of our highest nature, of which we now use only fractions, perhaps at moments in our lives. And some people don't even do that, isn't that so?

We're incipient human beings; we're on the way to becoming human.

If you want to say that a person becomes human the moment the atma-buddhi-manas link comes into existence, then we have to say that the soul is still an infant soul. It grows by experience through incarnation and through this long cycle of necessity, this enormous and very laborious process of self-growth, self-understanding, self-realization, as we ingest meaning out of our experience, learning the lessons of life—our soul building, if you want to put it that way.

The essence of an incarnation, its perfume, is an intangible quality that is never lost. That essence, that fragrance, comes from the trials and the tribulations that the individual undergoes in incarnation. It is that human being's offering to the whole of life, to the world, and to all other people. It is never lost. That achievement, that accomplishment, is the individual's mark of growth and enlightenment, but it is also the individual's contribution to the whole.

A long time ago in a meeting in Nairobi, where I was on a panel, a person asked me the question: Does God evolve? Nobody else wanted to address the question. And I said that of course it depends upon what you mean by "God." If by "God" you are referring to that ineffable reality that lies behind everything, that does not evolve because that doesn't change. But if by "God" you mean what most people mean by "God," the divine element in relationship to our world, then of course God evolves. God must evolve as the world evolves, because God is the soul of the world.

If you think of God in those terms, then God does evolve because the world evolves and the world is ensouled by God.

It may seem a contradiction. We say that the mineral monad overshadows maybe the whole of the earth, the mountains of the earth, everything that goes on in that realm, such as volcanic forces. Nevertheless, from one point of view, that monad can be called a human monad because eventually it has to pass through the stage of conscious self-direction or whatever a human being may be. Blavatsky goes on to say, "It ceases to be human only when it becomes *absolutely divine*" (2:185). To be divine is to transcend the world of change and experience.

There is no such thing as a Monad (jiva) other than divine, and consequently having been, or having to become, human. . . . It is divine in its higher and *human* in its lower condition—the adjectives "higher" and "lower" being used for lack of better words—and a monad it remains at all times, save in the Nirvanic state [when you go beyond]. As the Logos reflects the Universe in the Divine Mind, and the manifested universe reflects itself in each of its Monads, . . . so the MONAD has, during the cycle of its incarnations, to reflect in itself every *root-form* of each kingdom. Therefore, the Kabalists say correctly that "MAN becomes a stone, a plant, an animal, a man, a Spirit, and finally God. Thus accomplishing his cycle or circuit and returning to the point from which he had started as the *heavenly* MAN." But by "Man" the divine Monad is meant, and not the thinking Entity, much less his physical body. [2:185–6]

The Mahatma Letters (chronological ed. letter 70c; 3d ed. letter 20c) say, "Of course the Monad 'never perishes whatever happens.'" *The Secret Doctrine* has references to people who die and go to avichi (an unpleasant condition rather like hell). There's a lot about what happens to you if you don't fulfill your karma and so on. But what happens according to *The Secret Doctrine* is that the lower principles are severed from the higher and the lower principles are what perish. The Monad never perishes.

The spiritual ego is immortal in the sense that it persists from one to the other round. That is, between pralayas, it's immortal, but the personal ego does not survive. The monad is immortal but not the soul, which is the vehicle of the personal ego. Many personal entities blend into one individuality, the long string of lives emanating from the same immortal monad. And this is why people think that the atma or the spiritual self is way beyond us, without much relation to who we are or what we are. That isn't true. The atma, the monad, is present in us at all times, even when we are most unconscious of it, even when we are most misled as to what we are doing.

The link with the monad is never broken except deliberately by the individual. And such cases are what HPB means by *lost souls*, ones that go to avichi. Then that connection will be severed, and the monad just has to cut its losses and say, "Okay, I have to begin again." We may think that the monads are divine beings and therefore never make a mistake, but that's not true. We live in a world of change, of circumstances, all kinds of factors come to bear, and mistakes are made.

Even in the beginning, HPB says there were monads that were laggards, that didn't wish to become involved.

And you keep thinking, how could that be, why would a monad do that? There is an element of freedom, of choice, which is implicit in the human condition. The monad is called human because freedom of choice is inherent in the human condition. When we are denied that freedom, we may suffer under a loss of freedom for a generation or two generations. But all of a sudden, human beings can't stand it another minute, we're going to do something about it, and then we have a revolution, or we have a new paradigm, or we have a new religion.

Human beings have an innate drive to be free, to be self-determined. That is our necessity, born out of our very highest nature because when the sparks hang from the flame they are part of that flame. But the spark is also an incipiently free entity that will do something on its own. It'll light a fire here or there. The will-to-be is part and parcel of what the atma really is. I will to be myself, whatever that self may be. That is part of the world-creating drive, to create all the specificity, the uniqueness in nature. We could have had just one species of tree. But in fact we have many.

The star under which a human Entity is born, says the Occult teaching, will remain for ever its star, throughout the whole cycle of its incarnations in one Manvantara. But *this is not his astrological star*. The latter is concerned and connected with the personality, the former with the INDIVIDUALITY. The "Angel" of that Star, or the Dhyani-Buddha, will be either the guiding or simply the presiding "Angel," so to say, in every new rebirth of the monad, *which is part of his own essence*, though his vehicle, man, may remain for ever ignorant of this fact. [1: 572–3]

Thus the Monads when individualized are not separate but one in their essence with the Divine or Universal Monad. And this is not an impersonal entity. When HPB talks about the star or the angel or the Dhyani Buddha, she shows that it's not a cold or mechanical process. It's always imbued with a sense of individuality, of relationship, of warmth, of love, of connection, of intelligence. It's not a mechanical process at all.

I think it's like the Nirmanakaya vesture in Buddhism. Those monads who have evolved through a whole cycle of incarnation don't withdraw from the world and remain in Nirvana. They become active forces and establish nurseries in which the next evolutionary cycle will be fostered and will be aided.

This is why *The Secret Doctrine* says that evolution is a never ending process. Of course it's completely mind-boggling, and there's never any indication of when it began or where or when it will end. We don't know, because these are great mysteries. But it is said again and again that each new manvantara begins where the previous one left off. It's not just a repetitive process.

Each monad is said to be under one of the seven rays. The rays are very obscure and difficult to understand. HPB insisted always on a septenary system, so there are supposed to be seven rays. But how would any one of us know which ray our monad is under?

Even our observation of the world—our own experience—shows us that not all monads are at the same level or degree of development. This doesn't mean, as I said before, that any one monad is better than another monad. It's just that some of them have had less experience, haven't been in existence as long. Some have a different pace from others. How can we judge it? Time is meaningless in this context of eons of time.

As I have said, when I first became a member, there were many oversimplifications. Some Theosophists used to say, "Well, these are our younger brothers; they haven't quite evolved as far as we have. So we must be very charitable because these are our younger brothers." That really is offensive, is it not?

25. The Pilgrimage

I would now like to focus on the pilgrimage itself. We say that the monad has passed through all these kingdoms and thereby the kingdoms were established: the mineral, the vegetable, the animal—the world of nature—and also on the involuting arc, the mental and astral domains (kama-manas), and the etheric. These worlds have been created by the evolutionary process in which the monads have been engaged for eons of time.

So there is a world present for the human condition, although it is also said in *The Secret Doctrine* that the early races had a tough time because there were no proper physical bodies for human beings to inhabit. Therefore, the early human races were considered to be ethereal, gigantic, not very substantial, and obviously not very responsive to the inner life or the inner intent.

It was even difficult to discover processes of reproduction. Sexuality had not yet been created because there was so little substantiality. Nevertheless, there was this struggle of the monads to merge themselves with matter, to develop a form which could be self-expressive of life. This is why *The Secret Doctrine* insists that human beings occurred before the animals did.

Although the monads passed through a long previous cycle in the form of ensouling life that was of the nature of the animal world, as far as the individual is concerned, human beings really had to develop their own natures and their own constitutions. There was a big struggle, and it is said that many of the monads said, "I don't want to be bothered with that. I'm not going to do it. I'll wait until somebody else has laid the groundwork, and then I'll condescend to come." Now you think, "How would monads behave like that?"

Then HPB says other things about evolutionary streams, which are mentioned in various places in The *Secret Doctrine*, for example:

There exists in Nature a triple evolutionary scheme, for the formation of the three *periodical Upadhis*; or rather three separate schemes of evolution, which in our system are inextricably interwoven and interblended at every point. These are the Monadic (or spiritual), the intellectual, and the physical evolutions. [1: 181]

When HPB talks about the spiritual evolution of the monad, that almost seems like a contradiction in terms, for she says over and over again that the monad is eternal. When she says this, she means that all evolution is from "unconscious perfection" through "conscious imperfection" to "conscious perfection." In that sense, the monad evolves. The monad is unconscious on our plane; it is conscious of its own divine milieu, but not of anything else.

If the evolutionary scheme is summed up in those three phrases, it is the development of its conscious perception of what it really is, and that's not the same as intellectual development. It's a flowering of the spirit. The spirit exists always, latent, like a lake—a pool—which is there but in which nothing happens. And then the lake may be vivified with all kinds of life going on in it. It's the same lake, but it has a different relationship. HPB contrasts the spiritual development of the monad (which is really its flowering) with the intellectual evolution, which is represented by the Manasa Dhyanis, the givers of intelligence, the informational content of the whole world.

26. Evolution's Starts and Stops

As various people have said, evolution is a learning process, a process of trial and error. Nature is full of dead ends, things that were tried out but didn't work very well, and so were abandoned. Various species have died out. We may feel very sad about the fact of the vanishing of various species. However, from the long-term point of view, it really doesn't matter because life is going to persist and evolve other forms.

We tend to think that evolution is all in the past, that the whole process of evolution was to bring us to this point. Well, this point is a blink of an eye. Evolution will continue beyond this moment in time. It is not a process that has reached its culmination now. We are afloat on this river, and the river is continuing. So if species die out, it may be because they have outlived their usefulness, having achieved as much as they can in this stage of evolution.

When you think about it, an elephant is the quintessence of elephant. How could we get a higher form of elephant? And in a sense, the domestic animals have in a way reached their peak of beauty of form, of development, of quality of life, consistency and relationship, and all of that. If the form has attained its peak of usefulness, that's perfection. Could you think of a living form that would be more beautiful than a beautiful race horse, for example. It's a quintessence of that aspect of life which the horse displays.

The inwardness and the outwardness conform to each other in an almost magical way. It is the same with a running cheetah. The whole embodiment of what that creature is, its statement of self, is displayed in its action, in its behavior. In a sense it has reached a peak. What can happen to it? It can't go any farther forward in that form. But I think that, though we are not sentimental, we are full of sentiment and love and appreciation, and it breaks our hearts to think of anything dying. We have to remember what the Bhagavad Gita says: "I am not born, nor do I die." Forms come and go, but there is always the possibility of the creation of new forms.

27. The Immense but Finite Process

The Secret Doctrine describes in detail the evolution of the monads:

Then, again, another great perplexity was created in the minds of students by the incomplete exposition of the doctrine of the evolution of the Monads. To be fully realised, both this process and that of the birth of the Globes must be examined far more from their metaphysical aspect than from what one might call a statistical standpoint . . . for *outside* of metaphysics no occult philosophy, no esotericism is possible. It is like trying to explain the aspirations and affections, the love and hatred, the most private and sacred workings in the soul and mind of the living man, by an anatomical description of the chest and brain of his dead body. . . . As the evolution of the Globes and that of the Monads are so closely interblended, we will make of the two teachings one. . . . There must be a limited number of Monads evolving and growing more and more perfect through their assimilation of many successive personalities, in every new Manvantara. This is absolutely necessary in view of the doctrines of Rebirth, Karma, and the gradual return of the human Monad to its source—absolute Deity. Thus, although the hosts of more or less progressed Monads are almost incalculable, they are still finite, as is everything in this Universe of differentiation and finiteness. [1:169–71]

I think this is an interesting idea. HPB stated this before Einstein formulated his theory of the curvature of space and before our comprehension that, although the universe is gigantic, it is still finite. The universe has limits: it is not infinite in its capacity.

One of *The Mahatma Letters* (chronological ed. letter 62; 3d ed. letter 18) says, "Every Spiritual Individuality has a gigantic evolutionary journey to perform." The Master continues to describe how the monad, on each of the planets, has to pass through seven successive human races "up to the present *fifth* race, or rather variety, and through two more races, before he has done with this earth only; and then on to the next, higher and higher still."

So from *The Secret Doctrine*'s point of view, the Pilgrimage is an immense journey. Although we are supposed to be beyond the midpoint, we are just beginning the upward arc. Human beings are just beginning to be really self-determined, and not just creatures that are conditioned and conform and follow their impulses, creatures at the mercy of their own natures and dominated by their egotism.

28. Evolutionary Guides and Cycles

The Secret Doctrine says that teachers who are more highly evolved are sent to us. You can call them angels, rishis, great spiritual leaders, enlightened beings, incarnations, whatever you like, but they are sent to encourage human development. They are really the founders of the great religions, which were inspired. It may not be how we perceive them today, but if you go back to their origins, the great religions were all inspired. They were given to humanity by great beings who appeared from time to time to be exemplars.

Those great beings came to humanity to teach us what human beings can be and really are. Therefore, they are in a sense showing us what our future will be. That seems presumptuous in a way. However, the Buddha certainly taught that what he had accomplished, every human being can accomplish. And it is said that, during the time of his life, many did accomplish the same tasks by the inspiration of his presence.

The process of arriving at that future can be quickened. It doesn't have to be slow. I have a feeling that this quickening is occurring now. In fact, it is said in *The Secret Doctrine* and elsewhere that, as we are approaching not only the end of the century but the end of a millennium, we are coming to the end of a significant cycle. There is a quickening which I certainly think we can see around us. This century has been filled with more dramatic incidents and change than any other in history. It may be that many of us feel ourselves very fortunate that our karma has brought us into incarnation at this particular moment in time, when there is a kind of self-awakening in many human beings.

Time is purely relational. Of course, time is also celestial and terrestrial. Our time is built upon natural cycles, diurnal cycles and the annual circuit of the earth around the sun. These are established natural facts that we live with, and it doesn't matter whether we measure them in hours or minutes or some other form. Every culture has measured them in some way. But the fact of the matter is that things do go in cycles.

Whether we measure the peak of a cycle or the beginning of a new cycle or its nadir, whether it's going to be year

2000 or 2001—that doesn't really matter. It means that we have come to a point in our journey which has some significance. We can look at history only so far as we know it, which is just infinitesimal really; historical time is really a very tiny segment.

Obviously there have been big epochs. You might say that at the vanishing of the dinosaurs, something happened; nobody knows exactly what happened, though there are all kinds of theories. There obviously was a big transition some thousands of years ago when human beings really began to proliferate and the world became acculturated; before that it was much more a natural world. At this point, we can look at the population of the world, we can look at the condition of the world, and say we're getting to another crisis situation, where we're getting an awful lot of human beings. We're getting to be a critical mass.

Everyone is making predictions, but you have to take them with a big grain of salt. I don't think any of them have ever worked out—all the predictions about the end of the earth, comets coming, or something happening. All those predictions have proved empty. They are really representative of something going on in human beings. Some people love them. If they seem to us significant, they have some significance, isn't that so? Even if the reasons are not very good, something still has importance if human beings think it is so.

We know that the earth has gone through all kinds of phases in the past. There have been ice ages, tilting of the poles, the continents have changed, the climate has changed, everything has changed. That doesn't affect human beings; its all theoretical, it all happened way back then when we weren't around. It isn't affecting us now.

29. Change and the Changeless Now

We are interested in the immediacy of the moment. In some ways you may say that is stupid because, from *The Secret Doctrine*, we know we have been around a very long time. And yet this moment in time, this "now" is really the only slice of reality we have. "Now" is the vertical axis of human existence. This is the moment in which we can act. The past can't do anything about the future. The future is constantly receding, isn't that so? So in that way it is an imaginary quantity. "Now" is the only thing that has any reality. It is the timeless moment. It is of no duration. "Now" has no extension in time. "Now" is a dimensionless point. And that is what the monad is, a dimensionless point.

Change occurs, transformation occurs, illumination occurs, enlightenment occurs "now," and they also occur only in physical incarnation. I am fully convinced that the attainment of insight, nirvana, enlightenment, prajna, divine illumination, or whatever you want to call it has to be at a moment when we are fully conscious—when everything, all the elements of our being, are fully engaged. Then it comes through like a flash of lightning, and the transformation occurs. This is what happens in a genuine mystical experience, the kind of thing St. Francis had. It is like the butterfly bursting out of the chrysalis. All the elements were in the caterpillar. The elements are the same, but they have been transformed by the action of the divine impulse.

In one sense, time is irrelevant because when illumination happens, it happens in an instant, in a flash, in the twinkling of an eye. However, from another point of view, time is tremendously important, because we have to progress to that flash point. There is a long period of preparation for that moment of illumination. Everything has to be brought together, all the elements of our being have to be united for the sudden dissolution of the ahamkara, the ego. The barrier of the personal ego is penetrated or dissolved all at once. The higher self, the soul, then takes full command of all the elements of a human being. It happens instantaneously. When that happens, it is outside of time. It has nothing to do with time. It is eternity presenting itself.

Of course, you have to prepare for that moment, just as a violinist prepares for the perfect performance by practicing with the instrument. You can say the evolutionary process is the perfecting of the violin so that the sweet tone can make itself audible. That's a legitimate way to think of it. The gandharvas, the Hindu divine musicians, are everywhere, so the cosmos is filled with musical sound, but unless you have a medium you can't hear that sound. It has to be realized through its instrument, and the development of that instrument is a painstaking process. A musician has to learn his technique, otherwise he can't make his music audible. Maybe in his own head he can hear it, but nobody else can.

30. Limitations and Possibilities

Although the evolutionary process is a procedure through time, there is a vertical dimension and a horizontal dimension. We move through time, but that "connection," that other pole, that other dimension, is always present and available and accessible. Otherwise, to go through time would not be possible. The two have to come together to make up our three- or four-dimensional world. We live in a world that is conditioned or constructed in terms of these dimensions. Fritz Kunz always said that this is an "actuality," a physical reality that we sometimes take for granted because we are so accustomed to it.

It took a long time for a perfectly free spirit to become willing to imprison itself in the constraints of matter. We are hung on the cross of matter. We are terribly constrained by the limitations of our own physical bodies and the world we live in. We have to live in this tiny film that is the biosphere. We need certain conditions. We have to have air. And conditions of temperature have to be right for us. We can't live at great extremes of heat and cold. It is a very narrow and constrained world, but this is the world we have created for ourselves.

While our world is limited in one sense, in that it is a very narrow, viable space for us to live in, in another sense, it is totally limitless in its possibilities of what we can do in it. That is why small is wonderful. If we had infinite expansion as the monad has in its own sphere, we could not progress, because we need delimitation in order to accomplish things. We need structure. We need form. We need to appreciate the meaning of form, its role and function, and what constraints it places upon us.

Therefore, it is not just a question of the destruction of form, but a question of the transformation and the illumination of form. We need an appreciation of what form has accomplished. Without the building of form, we would have no world. There is in all of evolution a formative tendency to develop ever more beautiful, useful, responsive forms that encourage the flowering of all the qualities of spirit.

The Mahatma Letters insist upon delineation of the rounds and the races, the cycles of evolution, the globes, the chains, and the worlds. They insist that the human monad and the monad of the globe are the same thing. They want us to understand that the progression of human life and spiritual development is absolutely tied into the universal one. This concept is different from the biblical picture, where the world is created, and then human beings are created and put there to make use of the world, like a house that was built, after which we can move in and do anything we want to it. I think this is a misinterpretation of the Biblical story, but it has been a prevalent one—that nature is there for us to exploit. The concept that our evolution is inextricably tied to natural evolution is a different perspective.

31. Nature Unaided Fails

HPB called her commentary on stanza 2 of the second volume of *The Secret Doctrine* (2: 52), "Nature Unaided Fails." She repeats the idea several times, for example (1: 181), "'Nature.' the physical evolutionary Power, could never evolve intelligence unaided." Current belief is that nature slowly evolved a nervous system, a brain, and all of the complex biological systems out of simpler forms.

What are simpler forms? Now we are beginning to think that even at the most so-called primitive level very complex processes go on in creatures that don't have a brain or a spinal cord. Very complex procedures go on in insects and worms and fungi. The simple evolutionary view, which even mystical scientists like Teilhard de Chardin to some degree embraced, is that, as you go from the most primitive to the most complex, everything mounts and converges as it mounts. It's not that simple.

How nature produced a thing like the human brain is a tremendous mystery. How did it evolve? You might say there were certain requirements. Evolutionary theory really can't account for it. Scientists now talk about evolution by "punctuated equilibrium" or "transcendences." Big evolutionary leaps are made, in which something new has started, and you can't get the connection between the old and the new.

No connection has been made between the dinosaurs and the mammals. Why did the dinosaurs die out? We used to say that they were clumsy; and now scientists don't think that at all. The dinosaurs had brains, they were very mobile, they took care of their young, they had nests. It isn't true that they couldn't adapt, so what happened? We don't know. Maybe an asteroid hit us. But why didn't dinosaurs reappear? Why were they replaced by wholly new kinds of species? These are tremendous mysteries.

HPB says on this subject: Nature can't do it by herself. Nature has a degree of intelligence, but that intelligence comes from within. It does come physically from molecules sort of clumping together, and then after a while it seems as though a clump survives better than an unclump. It might never happen. It's like the monkeys and the typewriter.

There has to be a fusion of the inner and the outer in order for anything really to be accomplished. Science never took consciousness into consideration. You never found the word in any scientific discussion. It just didn't appear, just as nobody ever talked about life—they talked about living things, but they didn't talk about life. Consciousness and life were considered epiphenomenal. The physical body is a mechanical system. And mechanical systems do not survive unless energies are put into them. Otherwise entropy occurs, and they run down.

Living systems are not like that. Living systems have a constant infusion of . . . what? Something. And it's something intrinsic, not something that has been added. When HPB says that nature could never have evolved intelligence unaided, she is saying that intelligence is not a by-product of the brain, which is the most common theory today. But even today we see that certain areas of the brain are capable of doing certain things though nobody has any idea how or why.

People have thought that we could have artificial intelligence and that a computer could certainly mimic everything to do with the brain. Now people again need to respect the brain a great deal more than they once did. We have discovered that we use very little of the brain and that certain areas can learn to replace other areas removed by surgery or accident. Certain processes can be duplicated; other things are much more difficult to relearn—why is this? The whole relationship of brain and consciousness is coming to seem much more complex than we used to think it was.

Blavatsky says (1: 181–2):

"Nature," the physical evolutionary Power, could never evolve intelligence unaided—she can only create "senseless forms," . . . . The "Lunar Monads" cannot progress, for they have not yet had sufficient touch with the forms created by "Nature" to allow of their accumulating experiences through its means. It is the Manasa-Dhyanis who fill up the gap, and they represent the evolutionary power of Intelligence and Mind, the link between "Spirit" and "Matter"—in this Round.

The monads that began to inhabit this world had a previous cycle of existence on what is called the lunar chain, so are called "Lunar Monads." The "Manasa-Dhyanis" are beings at the level of Divine Intelligence. From this passage again we understand that the power of intelligence is an evolutionary force.

32. The Goal of the Pilgrimage

As I said before, we have to understand that fohat is a power. Love is a power. Intelligence is a power. It can do work. It can accomplish things. It is not just an emotion of feeling good, but a real power, a transforming power. The Dalai Lama is absolutely right when he says that if all human beings could feel compassion for one another, we would eliminate war, violence, and all of the social problems we have. When we say this, it sounds terribly simplistic. But when we realize that love is a power, it makes more sense. These powers have been gradually developed by human beings over the evolutionary period.

We are still at what I would say is just the midpoint of our development. HPB talks a lot about what the future will hold for us, about many more developments, for example, of what buddhi is. The major resource which the monad has for the human personality is the level of buddhi, the vesture of atma, through which one is able to have access to atma, which is not of this world.

The faculty of buddhi, which is the fundamental characteristic of the monad, and is perhaps the heart or focal point of the soul, makes it possible for the soul to perceive its relationship to the divine. Otherwise, there would be no possibility of our realizing our connection with it. The divine is not perceptible: you cannot taste it, or see it, or feel it. Yet all human beings are responsive to the idea that there is a divine or spiritual element in the world, though it has never been proven, never been seen, never been cognized, and every thing said about it has been wrong.

Nevertheless, buddhi—the illumination of buddhi, its shining upon the mind and through the mind—is that faculty, that vesture of the soul, which makes it possible for the mind to begin to understand our true nature and our links with the spiritual domain. When the mind turns itself towards the Self, there is a big transformation in the self. When the mind is open to insight, then you get wisdom, then you get prajna, enlightenment, illumination.

We know this is possible because we have the testimony of people, as well as our own very, very partial or momentary glimpses of what that kind of wisdom is. It transcends knowledge. It transcends information. It is a kind of light that illumines from above and makes a degree of clarity in our lives that is absolutely true for ourselves.

When we open ourselves to these influences, they become more and more real for us, because they are our own fundamental nature. Therefore, it is not anything that we are imagining; it is something which we gradually begin to realize or to appreciate as a presence in our lives. In our own deepest and highest moments of insight or truth, it becomes real for us.

The evolutionary task for humanity as spelled out in *The Secret Doctrine* is one of real glory. Even if progress is slow for some, who may spend life after life not making any real efforts to learn from experience, nevertheless, the evolutionary tide is going to make even the slothful ones gradually more and more able to apprehend what they really are.

The efforts that any single person makes toward that goal are not selfish. *The Mahatma Letters* stress this over and over again. The contributions that we make, the efforts that we make toward any tiny degree of spiritual insight, are not for our own personal self-development, but for humanity as a whole. This is the bodhisattva ideal. *The Mahatma Letters* invoke the great whole of humanity: the same compassion that we might feel for ourselves, we have to feel for others, and vice versa.

We are all engaged in the same great work. We are all walking on the same path. We are all seeking the same end, no matter how diverse our paths may be, and are enriched by the fact that so many people contribute from so many different points of view. All of these contributions go to enrich the whole of life for all of us.

So I would say that every Theosophist has to be an optimist, because we feel that nothing is lost, nothing is wasted. You do not have a wasted life. We judge so much on externals. We judge our own performances, and we are very self-deprecating. Very often we remember our failures much more than we remember our successes. But in a way, that is good, because we learn from our failures, and very often we don't learn anything from our successes. That is probably why our failures loom large to us, but we see them out of all proportion. We don't see or appreciate the changes that those failures have evoked in us. This may sound simplistic, but the Theosophical view of human nature and of the world is one of ever-increasing fulfillment.

Appendix A
Some Fundamentals of Theosophy

by Emily Sellon

1. The source and cause of all manifest being is one absolute unknown and unknowable reality: ultimate, ever-present, boundless and eternal, beyond both being and non-being.

2. The universe, or world of being, is a reflection of this timeless oneness expressing itself under two guises: as subject, unconditioned consciousness or spirit; and as object, root-substance or matter/energy. These are but polar aspects of the one reality.

3. Nondual and self-existent, consciousness and matter co-exist inseparably as the field of all conditioned being; they constitute the "cause of the world," the "one form of existence," which everywhere exhibits this fundamental polarity.

4. The dynamic polar relationship between spirit and matter imparts to the universe its fundamental, ever-present motion, whose ongoing character gives birth to time and instills a rhythmic order or periodicity. This manifests itself throughout nature as the space-time processes of birth and death, the cycles of growth and decay. It is the "great breath," the basic life-action of the universe.

5. The constant interaction of consciousness and matter creates a universe that is intelligent, forceful, and alive, for life or mind is the interface between spirit and matter. Spirit, matter, and life or mind constitute the universal trinity that creates and pervades the worlds; every particle of matter is imbued with life and mind: consciousness precipitated. Thus the universe is both intelligent and intelligible, self-ordering and formative or creative of outer forms in accordance with its innate rationality, known as "nous," "mahat," the divine or universal mind. This is the logos doctrine.

6. The natural unfoldment of the One into the many occurs hierarchically according to a harmonic principle whereby one becomes two and then three (while remaining itself always one); the intrinsic relationships within the three-in-one create a sevenfold order according to this harmonic principle: a, b, c, ab, ac, bc, abc. Such unfoldment (whereby "the incognizable Brahman exhibits aspects of itself") imparts to the worlds of form their mathematical, musical, and rational order: As above, so below.

7. The universal consciousness or spirit, which is the essence of all life, constitutes the point of individual consciousness or ultimate being in every person, our fundamental identity with the One or the All—for consciousness is a "singular of which the plural is unknown."

8. Humanity, being a microcosm of the universe, embodies all its elements and principles; for the individual self or spiritual consciousness, the law of periodicity creates the "cycle of necessity"—the pilgrimage of every self through

the worlds of form according to the cyclic process of involution and evolution.

9. This cyclic process is accomplished through the force, and according to the laws, of action or karma; it is a process that is self-determined and constitutes the basis of freedom within a universe of intelligent order.

10. The human pilgrimage takes us from our source in the One through our experience of the many—the multiplicity of separate lives or moments of existence, and the uniqueness of individual being—back to union with the One Divine Source. Our goal is thus to complete the cosmic cycle of manifestation in full conscious realization of our Self, no longer as polarized between spirit and matter, self and other, but as both all and one with the Source of all. This realization is known as Enlightenment.

Appendix B
Glossary

Absolute: A reality unconditioned by any reality other than itself and without any limiting attributes; an impersonal term for what is called *God* in the Western exoteric tradition. In Hinduism, it is called PARA-BRAHM(AN) or *paramatman* (supreme self or spirit).

Activity: As a characteristic of the LOGOS: the ability to act, the potential power to produce results; the function of FOHAT. Compare WILL and WISDOM.

Adam kadmon: In Kabbalah: the primordial human being, the archetype of humanity; an aspect of the third logos.

Agape: In Christianity, the love of God for humanity; unconditioned, altruistic human love.

Ahamkara: (Literally, I-maker) The sense of self-identity, the ego.

Antahkarana: The link between the higher and lower manas; the connection between the incarnating individuality and the incarnated personality.

Arupa: Formless or bodiless. The term especially applies to the three higher, unmanifested planes.

Atma, atman: The ultimate reality, as manifesting in individuated form or as immanent in the world. Universal spirit; the seventh principle. **Atmic.**

Atma-buddhi: The monad as a universal principle. It is individualized by manas (mind).

Avichi: Often equated with the Western hell, but more properly a state of physical existence in which the personality has been severed from its monadic source.

Bodhisattva: One who is on the way to becoming a BUD-DHA; specifically, one who delays realizing the freedom from limitations that results from enlightenment in order to help others who are still caught in the web of illusion. The **bodhisattva vow** is the intention not to enter nirvana until all beings can enter together.

Brahma: One of the persons of the Hindu trinity, the Creator.

Brahman: The all-pervading, self-existing reality; the cosmic unity; the imperishable source of all things; the ground of being. It is said to be either with qualities, **saguna brahman,** when it is that reality operating in the world, or without qualities, **nirguna brahman,** when it is the equivalent of PARABRAHM.

Buddha: Enlightened or awakened one, the title given to Siddhartha Gautama after his enlightenment; anyone who has achieved liberation from the illusion of separateness and realized insight into reality.

Buddhi: Intuitive insight. Universal soul, the sixth principle; the vehicle of ATMA, forming with it the MONAD. **Buddhic.**

Chain: A series of seven GLOBES which is the field for a phase of evolution. Our phase of evolution is proceeding on the Earth chain, of which our physical planet is the fourth globe.

Consciousness: One of the three basic aspects of all reality; spirit; the INWARDNESS. Compare ENERGY and FORM.

Cycle of necessity: The process of evolution, consisting of alternating MANVANTARAS and PRALAYAS, or incarnations. "Necessity" here refers to the karmic results that inevitably follow upon actions.

Deva: A celestial power or agent. The term is loosely used for beings of several different kinds. One use is for the DHYAN(I) CHOHANS; another is for beings in the ELEMENTAL KINGDOMS.

Dharma: A term rich with complex meanings, often translated "duty," its basic sense is "law," derived from the root *dhr* meaning "bear, carry, support, uphold," related to the English word *firm*. Each being has its own dharma **(swadharma)** which derives from its own essential reality or INWARDNESS.

Dhyan(i) chohan: (Literally, lord of meditation) A being in any of various stages of evolution beyond the human. As enlightened beings, they are the intelligent forces in creation, the builders of the universe, the agents of cosmic law. Collectively, they are the mind of the universe or the manifested LOGOS.

Dhyani buddha: One of seven advanced spiritual beings having oversight of the evolution of consciousness in one ROUND of an evolutionary system.

Elemental kingdom: One of three stages of evolution on the involving arc before the mineral.

Energy: One of the three basic aspects of all reality; that which relates CONSCIOUSNESS to FORM.

Eros: Love; desire. The Greek philosophers said there are two gods of that name: a terrestrial Eros, who is the god of sexual attraction and the life energy, and a celestial Eros, who is the god of divine love, which brings the universe into being.

Esotericism, esoteric science: Study of the inner, hidden nature of things, as distinct from the *exoteric* or outer appearance.

Etheric: Pertaining to a form of matter subtler than the dense physical that is perceptible to our ordinary senses. Also called *ethereal* or, in *The Secret Doctrine, astral* (a term used for the realm of desires or kama in later writings).

Evolution: The process of purposeful, directed change that all beings undergo in life. The whole **evolutionary** process consists of two phases or arcs, the first of which is INVOLUTION, and the second of which is called simply *evolution*. The term therefore denotes either the whole process generally, or specifically its second half, during which matter becomes more refined, awareness becomes more responsive, and consciousness or spirit becomes more unified. In the Hindu tradition, the latter is called *nivritti*, a "rolling out of (manifestation), back to (the source)."

Fohat: The energetic mutual relationship between consciousness and form, or the INWARDNESS and the OUTWARDNESS; love, EROS, awareness; an intelligent creative power; the one force that underlies all other forces in the universe.

Form: One of the three basic aspects of all reality; matter or substance; the OUTWARDNESS. Compare CONSCIOUSNESS and ENERGY.

Gandharva: A type of DEVA associated with music.

Globe: One of seven planets or spheres composing a CHAIN. The globes exist on four planes: two on each of the higher three planes, and the central globe of the seven on the lowest plane, so that the evolving wave of life manifests on a downward arc on the first three, reaches its nadir on the fourth, and continues on the upward arc on the last three globes.

Guna: (Literally, a cord or string for tying things together) One of the three basic qualities of matter: SATTVA, RAJAS, TAMAS, which are respectively harmony, activity, and entropy, and correspond to the INWARDNESS or CONSCIOUSNESS, FOHAT or ENERGY, and OUTWARDNESS or FORM.

Higher manas, higher mind: The pure mind, mental structure apart from any empirical content. As the vehicle of ATMA-BUDDHI, it individualizes the MONAD and thus is the basis of the reincarnating individuality. Also called the *causal body* or *buddhi-manas*.

Human monad: The MONAD manifesting through and individualized by HIGHER MANAS.

Immanence: The state of ultimate reality considered as existing within the PHENOMENAL world, contrasted with TRANSCENDENCE. Pantheism is the doctrine that ultimate reality is **immanent** only. Theosophy teaches that ultimate reality is both immanent and transcendent, a doctrine known as *panentheism*.

Involution: That phase of the whole EVOLUTIONARY cycle in which matter is becoming denser, awareness more restricted, and consciousness more fragmented. In the Hindu tradition it is called *pravritti*, a "rolling forth (from the source) to (manifestation)."

Inwardness: That aspect of being that is its nature in itself; CONSCIOUSNESS, spirit; one of the three basic aspects of being, along with OUTWARDNESS and their mutual relationship.

Jiva: Life. A term of varied uses. It sometimes denotes living, existing, being in a temporary state subject to the mutability of the empirical world, and the energy or PRANA that makes such living possible. But it also denotes the ABSOLUTE as IMMANENT in the PHENOMENAL world, and is used as a synonym for the MONAD.

Kama: Desire, eros.

Kama-manas: Mind linked to the principle of desire, *kama*. As such it is the empirical mind, expressing itself by a combination of feeling and thinking. Also called LOWER MIND, it is the seat of the personality and is the principle being especially developed in our period of evolution.

Karma: The principle of order in the universe; the law of cause and effect; the results that follow any action, especially the moral consequences.

Kingdom: One of the major stages of evolution. We experience directly four evolutionary kingdoms: mineral, vegetative, animal, and human. Preceding those are three ELEMENTAL KINGDOMS, and following them are three kingdoms of DHYAN CHOHANS.

Linga sharira: The subtle body that generates a new physical body. Also called ETHERIC or, in early literature, *astral* body.

Logos: (Literally, word) The creative and controlling power in the cosmos, described as threefold. The first or unmanifest logos is "the Mind of the Universe and its immutable Law," consisting of the potency for manifesting a universe. The second or manifesting logos is the actualizing energies of manifestation emanating from the first logos. The third or manifested logos is the collective body of DHYAN CHOHANS, who are the conscious embodiment of the LOGOS PRINCIPLE as its agents in the building of a cosmos. The characteristics of the logos are also sometimes called WILL, WISDOM, and ACTIVITY. Each subsystem of the cosmos also has its own logos.

Logos principle: The principle of awareness, order, law, which is IMMANENT in the universe; the cosmic intelligence, which is expressed in MANAS.

Lower manas: KAMA-MANAS.

Lunar monad: One of the beings that evolved on the (lunar) CHAIN previous to ours and that enter into our own evolutionary cycle. The several classes of lunar monads include beings who were in the animal or early human stages in the previous chain and are in the human stage, that is, are us, in our stage.

Man: Used alone and usually capitalized, *Man* may refer to the human archetype, ADAM KADMON or to the MONAD.

Manas: Mind, mental powers. Manas is considered to be twofold: HIGHER MANAS and LOWER MANAS, joined by the ANTAHKARANA. It is also said, however, that only one **manasic** principle exists, which functions in conjunction with BUDDHI or as KAMA-MANAS.

Manasa dhyani: One of the class of DHYAN CHOHANS that contributed the structure of the mind to human evolution. They are called by many names.

Manvantara: (Literally, the period of a Manu, or archetypal Man) A period of manifestation, contrasted with a PRALAYA.

Maya: The power to make reality appear other than it is. The **mayavic** world is the world of SAMSARA or of PHENOMENA.

Metaphysics: The basic principles on which one's view of oneself and of the world is based.

Mineral monad: The expression of the MONAD in the mineral stage, in which awareness is most restricted because its embodiment is most densely in matter. Between the mineral and the human stages, the monad's reflection is increasingly fragmented or individualized.

Monad: (Literally, unit or unity) The combination of ATMA-BUDDHI, which expresses itself through various forms in the evolutionary process. As the monad is expressed through increasingly denser forms of matter, it seems to be divided into separate entities, and is often so spoken of, although it remains ever whole on its own proper level. The monad is the PILGRIM in the evolutionary PILGRIMAGE.

Monadic essence: The monad considered as a unity, undivided in its evolutionary expressions, especially before the process of differentiation of consciousness begins in the vegetative stage of evolution.

Monas: (The nominative form of the Greek word from which *monad* is derived) The unmanifest first logos; the MONAD in its premanifested unity.

Mysticism: A direct perception of spiritual reality or the INWARDNESS, with a loss of one's personal ego through an experience of oneness with the whole universe and the ultimate ground of being. Contrasted with OCCULTISM.

Nirmanakaya: The state of those (that is, BODHISATTVAS) who have completed the human evolutionary stage but have elected to remain in our world in order to assist with the evolution of those in earlier stages. Making this choice is referred to as assuming the **nirmanakaya vesture.**

Nirvana: (Literally, blown out, extinguished) The extinction of the illusive sense of separateness; the state of enlightenment; a correct perception of reality, as distinct from SAMSARA. There are not two realities, but only one, which can be viewed in two ways; hence it is said that nirvana and samsara are the same.

Noumenon: (Plural, **noumena**) The full reality of a being as distinct from its mayavic or PHENOMENAL appearance in space and time. **Noumenal.**

Occultism, occult science: A study and perception of the reality of forms or the OUTWARDNESS. The current use of the word for a variety of practices loosely characterized as "magical" has interfered with its older use denoting a way of perceiving reality complementary with that of MYSTICISM.

Outwardness: That aspect of being that is its contact with others; FORM, matter; one of the three basic aspects of being, along with INWARDNESS and their mutual relationship.

Parabrahm(an): The ABSOLUTE, which under the influence of MAYA appears as the primal INWARDNESS and OUTWARDNESS, or the root of CONSCIOUSNESS and FORM.

Paranirvana: The state of fullest awareness of reality, of the ABSOLUTE; hence, the goal of the PILGRIMAGE.

Phenomenon: (Plural, **phenomena**) The appearance of a being in the MAYAVIC world of SAMSARA as distinct from its NOUMENAL reality. **Phenomenal.**

Physical body: The vehicle or OUTWARDNESS of all the other human principles.

Pilgrim: The MONAD in its role within the evolutionary process.

Pilgrimage: The evolutionary experience of the MONAD.

Prajna: (Literally, wisdom) The direct perception of reality; intuitive recognition of ultimate truth; gnosis.

Pralaya: (Literally, the process of melting, dissolution) The period of quiescence between two MANVANTARAS or periods of manifestation.

Prana: (Literally, breath) The vital energy of the body; one of the human principles.

Principles, human: The seven aspects, faculties, or components of human nature. The principles can be viewed as states of consciousness, as bodies or forms, or as types of energy. They are variously listed, for example as ATMA, BUDDHI, MANAS (sometimes divided into HIGHER MANAS and LOWER MANAS), KAMA (or KAMA-MANAS), LINGA SHARIRA, PRANA, and the PHYSICAL BODY.

Quaternary: A group of four things; specifically, the four lower principles.

Race: ROOT RACE.

Rajas: The middle of the three GUNAS; activity, energy, creative force; associated with BRAHMA and FOHAT.

Rishi: A seer, a holy wise man.

Root race: One of seven major stages of human evolution on our GLOBE in the present ROUND. Humanity is now in its fifth such root race. The term *race* or *root race* should not be confused with the common use of *race* to refer to a physical subtype of the present human species; it denotes rather the variety of consciousness, awareness, and form during an evolutionary stage of very long duration.

Round: An evolutionary period of development consisting of one passage of the life wave (or the MONAD) through all seven GLOBES of a CHAIN. The full evolution on a given chain consists of seven such rounds.

Rupa: Form, shape. The rupa worlds are the various states of manifestation.

Samsara: The cycle of birth and death; hence the MAYAVIC or PHENOMENAL world of change and impermanence, in which we function as ignorant and selfish beings, contrasted with NIRVANA. **Samsaric.**

Sattva: One of the three GUNAS; luminosity and intelligence; the centripetal force of cohesion; associated with VISHNU and INWARDNESS or consciousness.

Seven rays: Seven lines of development followed by manifestation. These rays have correspondences with the seven PRINCIPLES, ROUNDS, ROOT RACES, DHYANI BUDDHAS, and so forth. Each person is also said to be "on" one of the seven rays.

Shiva: One of the persons of the Hindu trinity; the destroyer, regenerator, or transformer.

Tamas: One of the three GUNAS; darkness, disintegration, inertia; the centrifugal force of dispersion; associated with SHIVA and OUTWARDNESS or matter.

Tao: (Literally, the way) A Chinese term corresponding approximately to DHARMA or the LOGOS PRINCIPLE.

Transcendence: The state of ultimate reality considered as beyond all PHENOMENA, contrasted with IMMANENCE. The **transcendent** reality is unknown and unknowable.

Upadhi: (Literally, vehicle) That by which any reality manifests or expresses itself; the OUTWARDNESS of any INWARDNESS.

Upanishad: (Literally, sitting down beside a teacher) A philosophical text imparting esoteric knowledge. The upanishads are seminal sources of Hindu philosophy.

Vishnu: (Literally, pervader) One of the persons of the Hindu Trinity, the preserver, the embodiment of goodness and mercy, who descends to earth from time to time, for example as Krishna, Buddha, etc.

Will: As a characteristic of the LOGOS, the intention to be, the expression of INWARDNESS; the DHARMA of a being. Compare WISDOM and ACTIVITY.

Wisdom: As a characteristic of the LOGOS, its OUTWARD-NESS, as ATMA is embodied in BUDDHI. Compare WILL and ACTIVITY.

Appendix C
Questions

These questions are open-ended, but their numbers correspond to those of the sections in the book.

1. How would you distinguish between the "metaphysics" and the "machinery" of Theosophy?

2. What are some implications for daily living of assuming that what is real and important is (a) the spiritual, (b) the physical, or (c) a unity embracing the spiritual and physical?

3. In what ways are all human beings the same, and in what ways are we each different?

4. What are the implications for living of either of these intents: to be free from reactive behavior or to dedicate oneself to the welfare of others?

5. In the cycles of our life, some phases appear to be regressions. What are some examples?

6. What do you understand by the terms "transcendence" and "immanence"? (A dictionary may help.)

7. What active powers do all human beings have, and what powers are latent in most of us but may develop?

8. In our own lives, in what ways do our "inwardness" (or consciousness) and our "outwardness" (or body and environment) affect each other?

9. What are some examples of fohat, or the power of interaction, operating on various levels—physical, emotional, mental, and spiritual?

10. Why do you suppose the One expresses itself as the many, and why is creative choice necessary for that expression?

11. What are some ways our behavior as human beings is like that of other forms of life, and what are some ways we are uniquely different?

12. How are the logos and the monad parallel?

13. How are the members of these pairs "inward" and "outward" of each other: atma/buddhi, manas/kama-manas, and prana/linga sharira, or all of those and the physical body?

14. Think of a thing or a change you do not like, and then consider how it fits into the order of the universe.

15. Do you know of a situation in which a person has intentionally made a change that deeply affected the course of that person's life?

16. Think of some artists, philosophers, scientists, or sages whom you know something about. To what extent do they seem to you to be mystics or occultists?

17. In what ways are form, energy, and consciousness different aspects of the same reality, and how do we experience various worlds (or levels) of them?

18. How is the human stage critical for evolution?

19. What are some ways in which humanity is an evolutionary force?

20. Is there one monad, or are there many? How might the answer to that question bear on the questions of whether some souls are "in advance" of others, of

whether "new souls" are coming into existence, and of how there can be more people living now than earlier?

21. What is meant by involution?

22. Why is an understanding of the mineral monad important?

23. What is the source of the monad, and why is that source important to our personal lives?

24. If we are only incipient human beings, what are the qualities of a fully human being?

25. A pilgrimage has a goal. What is the goal of the evolutionary pilgrimage?

26. What light does a Theosophical view of personal life and general evolution throw on personal death and the extinction of species?

27. How is the Theosophical concept of an immense but finite universe and evolutionary process like and different from scientific and religious views?

28. What changes in life today might suggest that we are living in a time of major transition?

29. If the "now" is all important and time is irrelevant, why does *The Secret Doctrine* talk so much about the past?

30. What is the value of limitations?

31. If nature unaided fails, what helps nature to succeed?

32. Why is every Theosophist an optimist?

Appendix D
Works for Further Study

H. P. Blavatsky's *The Secret Doctrine* is the basic text on the Pilgrim and the Pilgrimage. Several good editions are available, each having its own advantages:

The Secret Doctrine. 3 vols. Ed. Boris de Zirkoff in the Blavatsky Collected Writings series. Adyar, Madras: Theosophical Publishing House, 1978–79. Pp. [2], 84, xlvii, 696 + xxiv, 817 + vii, 520. Quest Theosophical Heritage Classics edition, 1993. Boxed paperback. [This is the best edition for students because it includes introductory matter, explanatory notes, and appendices helpful for an understanding of the book's content and background.]

The Secret Doctrine. 2 vols. Photographic facsimile of the 1888 edition. Pasadena, CA: Theosophical Univ. Press, 1988. Pp. xlvii, 676 + xvi, 798, [2], xxxi. [This is a well-printed and bound reproduction of the book as first published by Blavatsky.]

The Secret Doctrine. 1 vol. Facsimile of the 1888 edition, 2 vols. bound in 1. Los Angeles: Theosophy Co., 1947. Pp. [4], xlvii, 676 + xvi, 798, [2], xxx. Supplemented by *Index to The Secret Doctrine.* Los Angeles: Theosophy Co., 1939. Pp. x, 172. [This is a handy one-volume reproduction of the original edition on thin paper.]

An Abridgement of The Secret Doctrine. Ed. Elizabeth Preston and Christmas Humphreys. Wheaton, IL: Theosophical Publishing House, 1983. Pp. xxxii, 260. [This abridgment prints the Stanzas and their commentaries, but omits much of parts 2 and 3 of both volumes, dealing with mythology and especially science.]

Other works by H. P. Blavatsky that complement *The Secret Doctrine*'s presentation of the story of the Pilgrim and the Pilgrimage include these:

Collected Writings. Ed. Boris de Zirkoff. 14 vols. Wheaton, IL: Theosophical Publishing House, 1966–85. [The standard edition of Blavatsky's periodical writings.]

Collected Writings: Cumulative Index. Vol. 15 of the Collected Writings, comp. Boris de Zirkoff. Ed. Dara Eklund. Wheaton, IL: Theosophical Publishing House, 1991. Pp. xiii, 633. [An indispensable tool for serious study.]

H.P.B. Teaches: An Anthology. Comp. Michael Gomes. Adyar, Madras: Theosophical Publishing House, 1992. Pp. viii + 579. [A useful anthology of Blavatsky's writings.]

The Key to Theosophy. Photographic reproduction of the original edition of 1889. Los Angeles: Theosophy Co., 1962. Pp. xii, 310. [Blavatsky's presentation of her ideas to the inquirer.]

The Key to Theosophy: An Abridgement. Ed. Joy Mills. Wheaton, IL: Theosophical Publishing House, 1992. Pp. xv, 176. [A condensed version of Blavatsky's introductory book.]

The Voice of the Silence, Being Chosen Fragments from the "Book of the Golden Precepts." For the Daily Use of Lanoos (Disciples). Facsimile reprint of the original edition of

1889. With an introduction, "How *The Voice of the Silence* Was Written" by Boris de Zirkoff, and an index. Wheaton, IL: Theosophical Publishing House, 1992. Pp. 40a, xiv, 122. [A guide to the spiritual life emphasizing the next stage in human evolution, the bodhisattva path.]

Some works that are helpful companions to the study of *The Secret Doctrine* are the following:

Abdill, Edward C. *Foundations of the Ageless Wisdom: A Study Course to Accompany the Five-part Video Series "Foundations of the Ageless Wisdom."* Wheaton, IL: Olcott Institute, Theosophical Society in America, 1996. Pp. 24. Video length, 2½ hours.

Algeo, John. *Getting Acquainted with "The Secret Doctrine": A Study Course.* 2nd ed. Wheaton, IL: Olcott Institute, Theosophical Society in America 1995. Pp. 64.

Barborka, Geoffrey A. *The Divine Plan: Written in the Form of a Commentary on H. P. Blavatsky's Secret Doctrine.* Adyar, Madras: Theosophical Publishing House, 1961, revised 1964. Pp. xxvii, 564.

———. *The Peopling of the Earth: A Commentary on Archaic Records in The Secret Doctrine.* Wheaton, IL: Theosophical Publishing House, 1975. Pp. xiv, 233.

———. *The Story of Human Evolution: Written in the Form of a Commentary on The Stanzas of Dzyan—Second Series.* Adyar, Madras: Theosophical Publishing House, 1980, c. 1979. Pp. x, 147.

Cranston, Sylvia. *HPB: The Extraordinary Life and Influence of Helena Blavatsky, Founder of the Modern Theosophical Movement.* NY: Putnam's, 1993. Pp. xxiv, 648.

Hanson, Virginia, ed. *H. P. Blavatsky and The Secret Doctrine.* 2nd ed. Wheaton, IL: Theosophical Publishing House, 1988. Pp. xvii, 240.

McDavid, William Doss. *An Introduction to Esoteric Principles.* 2nd ed. Wheaton, IL: Olcott Institute, Theosophical Society in America, 1990. Pp. ix + 82.

Preston, E. W. *The Story of Creation According to The Secret Doctrine.* Adyar, Madras: Theosophical Publishing House, 1947. 2nd rev. ed. 1968. Pp. xii, 109.

——. *The Story of Man According to The Secret Doctrine.* Adyar, Madras: Theosophical Publishing House, 1949. Pp. x, 65.

Warcup, Adam. *Cyclic Evolution: A Theosophical View.* London: Theosophical Publishing House, 1986. Pp. [viii], 144.

Wood, Ernest. *A "Secret Doctrine" Digest.* Adyar, Madras: Theosophical Publishing House, 1956. Pp. xiv, 480.

THEOSOPHICAL SOCIETY IN AMERICA
P. O. Box 270
Wheaton, IL 60189

Dear Fellow of the
Theosophical Society:

The enclosed book, *The Pilgrim and the Pilgrimage*, by Emily B. Sellon, is the first volume in our new Theosophical series, Wisdom Tradition Books.

It is sent to you as a gift to introduce the new series and to celebrate the life and example of Emily, one of our most loved and inspiring fellow students.

This gift is made possible through the generosity of John Sellon and his sons, Peter, Jeffrey, and Michael, in memory of their wife and mother.

I know you will find the book both instructive and inspirational, like all of Emily's work.

Fraternally,
John Algeo
National President